D1029806

STEPHEN POTTER

POTTER ON AMERICA

RUPERT HART-DAVIS
SOHO SQUARE LONDON
1956

PRINTED AND BOUND IN ENGLAND
HAZELL WATSON AND VINEY LTD
AYLESBURY AND LONDON

TO

H

Introduction

WHEN I was a boy the United States seemed to me the most romantic and desirable place in the world. This was before the First World War, and in those days America was much farther away than it is now and seemed full of attractive mysteries. There were, for instance, a lot of funny little black-and-white people moving energetically about. Early films taught me that these jerky and excited motions must be normal in America. Perhaps they were having a good try at being as dignified and successful as the British. Besides these lovable dwarfs, I knew there were slow, manly men who lived in shacks in constant danger of attacks from Red Indians. The first full-length novel I ever read was about Indians—*The Headless Horseman*, by Mayne Reid. It took me ten months, not merely because reading was difficult, but because each chapter seemed to open the door wider to the dangerous but reviving winds of real life. So it seemed to a town-bred boy. *Huck Finn* gave me almost more pain than pleasure. I used to read it when I was getting better from colds or measles—when my love of being petted by my mother was superseded by irritation at her fussy intrusions on my desire to be a man. "Wrap up warmly when you go out, darling." I could hear it coming. "Your coat *and* your scarf." This to me, the friend of Huck—Huck, who by the Mississippi never even wore a jacket, but always the same tattered shirt, open to the great buckle of his belt. Because it was remote the flavour was not less sharp—the taste above all of openness and wildness. I did not know then that Britain contained places as wild and lonely as anywhere in the world. To me England was a walled garden, with nothing much wilder than the chalk pit, fascinating as that was, which so thrillingly changed the note of the L.B. & S.C.R. railway line, as we passed alongside it, just short of Upper Warlingham Station. The Americans seemed manly and wonderful. They were brave and successful in their wars, as we were; and they made a jolly good shot at trying to play our games, although of course they never won anything.

Now it is all different. The United States are not remote at all, but sitting on our front parlour window-sill, half-obscuring the view. I realised when at last my chance of a visit came that it was going to be more difficult to find the romance, or at any rate the strangeness. One of the great arts and trades of the United States is self-presentation—the self-portrait, made up of the aptly chosen detail, in the kind of film or magazine article which is very inappropriately called "documentary." The difficulty, when you first get there, is to see the panorama behind Cinerama, the life behind *Life*, and the glories of America behind the celestial male voice choir chanting these glories in unison. Another great difficulty is easiness. After transatlantic coddling comes the air hostess proffering glucose, or the still more relaxing "roomettes" of American railway travel. In the hotels we swallow large helpings of air specially cooked and refined; or velvety cars whisper us to a pampering country club. It is over such dire safeties and softships as these that the traveller in America must learn to triumph.

Even if he fails, what a pleasant time he will have. I have this also to say. My book is a diary of the two visits I made to America in 1955. On one of them my observation was sharpened and my enjoyment heightened by the presence of the companion to whom this book is dedicated; on the other, I paid my way by lecturing. I have read painful confessions of subservience to the "lecture racket," of lecturers who come back dazed with too much entertainment, endlessly meeting new people, bewildered by hotels, their personalities homogenised under a hardened and defensive exterior, like custard with crust on it, by American travel and parties and food, all for the packet of dollars. I can't compete with these revelations. So far as dollars are concerned, not being a very famous lecturer I barely broke even. As for the other things, I like lecturing and seeing new people, and never in my life have I been entertained half or lionised one-quarter as much as I would like to be. Taking it all in all, the romantic flavour of America was quite as strong as I imagined it would be, round about 1911. It was only the flavour of the romance which was not quite what, in those days, I had expected.

I would like to thank Rupert Hart-Davis for being invaluably helpful, as usual, in at least five different ways, during the preparation of this book.

S. P.

PART ONE

Spring 1955

9th March. Good. I am leaving England, and on the way to the U.S. There is a lot of liner beneath my feet—the most solid thing in the world when it is by the dockside. I am staring over the rail, down at the strip of water between the side and the dock. "Ruined clump water ——" I want to make up a Mr. Polly word for it. There is always something like an old railway-sleeper, or dished-up old straw, floating in it. I stare with a day-dreamy eye. (Impossible to believe that this weak stuff supports this mass of cliff and turret I am standing on.) The air journey to New York screws you up tight; the sea journey, on the contrary, unwinds you from the start.

I wanted unwinding, not only because tendons were strung up as tight as bones with harrowing personal events of the last year (all enacted—minor point—in thirteen months of the cruellest stretch of weather I remember), but also because H. was with me and I wanted to show her that, where journeys were concerned, I could casually take charge and be more clear and definite than she ever dreamed of. I am hoping to make use of her eyes, decidedly larger, brighter, and more wide-awake than my own, to help me with the business of seeing the U.S. It is not quite my first visit, but I shall still be partly in the stage of crossing things off.

We have both always been perfectly prepared to say "I lived there" even if it is only half an hour at the airport changing planes.[1] But truthfully of course it is impossible, on first acquain-

[1] Later in the year, flying the Atlantic, I certainly lived in Iceland, for instance. That was for twenty-eight minutes, refuelling. In accordance with the recommendations of my technique, I stooped down as I crossed the grass of that dark and chilly airstrip and picked a scrap of groundsel, sticking it between the pages of my diary. Afterwards I was able to take out this bit of groundsel and say: "I found this species of *Senecio* growing quite plentifully on flat ground in Southern Iceland."

tance, to "see" even the natural configurations of a new place. A sensitive nature artist usually scrapes off any canvases he has painted during the first weeks of a visit. In a place like New York City, particularly, one is "crossing off" for days—relieving the quiet but chronic irritation of personal ignorance of the Celebrated Object. "There *is* Brooklyn Bridge," you say, and a small boil, at last, bursts behind your left ear. "Yes—the Chrysler Building is the Chrysler Building," and a nail works out of your shoe. But what you are really seeing on the first days in New York are those old props you have been carrying about in the Gladstone-bag part of your mind for years, picked up from films, half-understood O. Henry stories, old magazine articles on waterfronts or 42nd Street or Mayor La Guardia. You are unpacking your pre-conceptions and looking at *them* again.

My first visit was in 1951. *Gamesmanship* had been published in New York, so I had the (financially essential) business reason or going. Already the fact that this book had a sprinkling of readers in the States increased for me the romance of, and gave even a touch of reality to, such names, such faceless images of foreign-ness, as Salt Lake City, St. Louis, Chicago, Iowa, Minneapolis. Stronger even than an author's desire to make a living is his desire to make links with the unknown and unseen reader; but if the tentacles are tied to something called *Sacramento* or *Medicine Hat*, one grips the world, surely, pretty well like an octopus.

*   *   *   *

I have got the Diary of this 1951 visit with me. I want to remind myself.

By the first entry I had already, I guess, got through the Empire State Building stage, and was crossing off things I had only heard of about half a dozen times already. Such as:

That U.S. Newspapers are Bigger

10th *May* (1951). My fifth day in New York is typical. I am staying at the Harvard Club. The Harvard Club is rightly regarded as fairly

English in atmosphere—and indeed there are enough dark corners, good solid waiters, and aloof gentlemen behind newspapers to make it a sort of oak-panelled rabbit-hole where I can stoke up on the customary before baring myself to the next batch of strange sights. Get up at 8.50, which just gives me time to get the Harvard Club English breakfast *plus* grapefruit-juice served in a sort of film-star's foam-bath of crushed ice—half a pint, not two drops squeezed out into a sticky thumb-glass. The morning paper is so huge that I have time to read only the start of five stories on the front page and haven't the eyesight, the time, or the detective skill to turn to p. 63, column 7, to follow them up. Reading these papers is like trying to read a feather-bed, so as a result I am almost completely ignorant of American news (let alone English)—except of how former N.Y. Senator showed his doggedness, courage, and indifference to the twists of fate when he received unflinchingly prison sentence of five years for supplying bribable Fire Brigade President with alternate blondes and brunettes, and how fourteen wealthy girls in the eighth grade (top form of High School) did not change colour when they were indicted on heroin charges.

That the U.S. are Bad at Maps

I try to buy a map of the U.S. for my route. The regular maps on sale are indecipherably pock-marked with a million names, and are totally without those revealing blues and greens and browns which enable one to have a faint idea of rivers and a height or two. The U.S. people—most surprisingly for a nation of nomads and trailer-folk—have not yet acquired the taste, so universal among Englishmen, for the well-spaced detail of our Ordnance inch-mile map, nor for the beautiful bird's-eye view given by Bartholomew half-inch. In fact I hardly found an American who knew which watershed he was in, which left me, as an Englishman who is uneasy unless he knows which ocean will finally receive his urination, scandalised.

Since the U.S. is practically uncharted, I recommend buying (a) a jigsaw puzzle of the U.S., each State one piece, because State position and State shape is the essential first lesson, and (b) the quite good State maps which, by some fortunate thrust of salesmanship, are given away free by an oil company.

That U.S. Radio is Casual and Unceasing

Almost daily, on instruction from Holt's (my publisher), I do a piece of Radio or TV. Today was the Stella Stow Radio Hour. I go to one of a dozen radio stations . . . just a segment of sky-scraper . . . go up in an express lift which makes me deaf . . . then a girl with trained sympathetic voice, but genuinely sympathetic also, puts me at a studio table with Stella, whose voice is as warm and easy as bedsocks; and she says she is going to talk to me with gramophone records interposed.

Though still sleepy and ears queer, I come out rather well in this interview, because she is genuinely easy to talk to, and having as usual the sense amounting to certainty that nobody is listening to me anyhow, I am not microphone-self-conscious. She has a surprisingly detailed dossier of Potter information, including my lightning appear-ance in the Coldstream Guards, which I have always felt a shade too brief to justify a *Who's Who* mention.

"I expect you feel worried about him and proud of him at the same time?"

"Who?"

"Your son in Korea——"

"Yes."

"Mr. Potter's son Julian—and this will interest you, as you pause in your small household jobs, I know—is fighting side by side with some of your boys in the Far East. Now it's all yours, Harry."

Then Harry at another mike says: "And don't forget Fortescue's Distempers are sold in nearly two hundred pastel shades and one of them is sure to please YOU."

Stella Stow leans over and whispers to me: "You don't mind me saying that, but political. You know. Show the British are in Korea." "Perfectly all right," I say. Stella: "Now tell me exactly, how do you say 'Bad luck' when you want to put your golf opponent off? Will you illustrate it?"

That Martinis are Strong

12th May. U.S. food seems to be superior to G.B.—better served and certainly better vitamined—on the Express-Dairy-A.B.C. level. There is also much more of it. Cheap restaurants usually seem to be part of a manicure establishment or along one side of a general grocery. At the moment I am sitting, with my diary, on top of everything in New York City except the top of the Empire State—on the flat parapet above the R.C.A. Building, the Rockefeller.

I got to know and love this Rockefeller Centre. The Empire State has a mean, fidgety pinnacle; the Chrysler is Cocktail Quinze—but the Rockefeller was the first to make me realise that this style of modern architecture could have proportions not less subtle, because they are simpler, than St. Paul's. The fact also that the main tower is in a proportioned group of skyscrapers somehow makes it friendly and amenable, instead of exhibiting, like most of them, a frowning precipice, uninhabited even by birds and therefore more grim than Cape Wrath. It may be this friendliness or tangible personality, or it may be some arrangement of railings on top, which makes it possible for me to sit there without a whisper from that insanity box buried somewhere in my mind which still sometimes repeats to me, "Jump over. Easy." I sit and write a lot up here.

12th May (continued). If I am beginning to understand American food, I still have not organised my American drinking. What to do about these drinks—the stronger, larger gins . . . and this business of the vermouth just rinsed round the glass and poured away again. One is really drinking double neat gin, double English strength. Whisky is safer, of course; but I don't really like whisky. Everybody warned me about it, but this hospitality and lack of sweat-producing exercise is getting me down. I have practically banned myself lunchtime apéritifs. But take this evening. At 5.15 (no off-drink hours here) I was (first of all) guest of some of the editorial board of *Fortune* at the Algonquin Hotel, a sort of Savage-Club-in-Adelphi-days meeting-place, with tables where, e.g., Benchley once sat, and though such rendezvous are in a permanent state of having lost something of their old magic, the something is permanently there. Five young men, well up in games-lifemanship, wanted to discuss with me gambits for *Businessmanship*. We worked out in useful detail such ploys, for instance, as the one-downness of having a small desk, smaller carpet, smaller room. They told me of the bold counter by K, who got the workmen in at night to shift his partition so as to make his room larger than J's. This hierarchical behaviour is more common here than in London. Then there is R. D. Pollinger, champion in what I taught them and they taught me was Mistakemanship—the taking of wrong, if minor, decisions in order to admit later, in a softly reverberating voice, that they were wrong decisions. Then there is my gambit for chief ex-ecutive—having *nothing* on his desk *at all*. They tell me of Fred Wilkie who has one small empty desk and *one* telephone across the room which he *gets up to answer*. Shaver of Lord & Taylor [1] has no desk at all. Mr. Henry Luce is just called "Editor." Only those *below* the high-ups who work with him can call him "Harry." This manshiply discussion gave me material for a useful chapter. I hope it was useful to my kind hosts.

After Gibsons at the Algonquin, and signing books for these high-ranking young men and having signed books given to me, I felt warmed and relaxed and all ready for my next date, 6.15 at the Twenty One Club. This large and fairly expensive restaurant ("Club") has a broad curved bar like the bridge of a liner. It has romantic associa-tions with the height of the speakeasy period, and I was rather given to understand that by pressing a button the whole bar could still be made to turn on its axis like a revolving stage to reveal a Salvation Army meeting, with trombones, singing *Rock of Ages*. Here I was guest of Ted Patrick, a great name in U.S. editing, though I am only just beginning to know and appreciate his *Holiday*. He offered me a good fee for a "Travelship" article if only I can get round to thinking of ideas for it. Fame is much more attainable for me here than fortune. Ted owes his success to being a soft-boiled executive, getting things done because he is kind and perfectly con-siderate. With him was sweet, white, bald, protoplasmic, electric-eel Jerry Weidman, the novelist, type of a lost type in England, the witty cause of wit—or at any rate he is funny in conversation. Instead of making a platitude of a situation, as do some rich-voiced Americans, he enucleates the *non sequitur* of it. I started off by saying: "I think your taxi-drivers are the salt of the earth." [2]

---

[1] Lord & Taylor is expensive Fifth Avenue shop, with rather dramatic dis-play styles. One looks through the window at, apparently, a preview of modern paintings full of smart women. But the smart women are dummies, wearing Lord & Taylor hats and beautiful shoes and stockings. Of American *chic* more later; but (strong contrast with Europe 1951, except Italy) they tend to be smart in their extremities. Four-fifths of visible women everywhere seem to have grade A nylons. Chic or dowdy, the nylons are good. But here is where those precisely graded subdivisions of the central section of Manhattan show most clearly. In Fifth Avenue the nylons in shops and on legs have no darker inset heels. In Sixth a very small inset. On Broadway (next west) a long dark inset to above the ankle. On Seventh the heel is loudly meshed. On Eighth Avenue it is boldly diagonalised. On Ninth all sorts of things happen, including crossed hearts or "guess my number" worked into the calf.

[2] They are. I have long conversations with all my taxi-drivers, trying to make my voice as deep and friendly as theirs. A remark that succeeds with them is to

All agree everybody has to say this or be branded as a bad democratic mixer.

We talk about Philadelphia. Everybody runs down Philadelphia apparently. It has a bad water-system. Its river is dirty. "The people walk slow, one-two, one-two (*Weidman imitating with fingers*), two or three people abreast."

PATRICK: There was a cop with his tunic unbuttoned smoking a pipe. They're all political appointments.

WEIDMAN: They look all right, but they're just appointments. It's like the television record of the Kefauver corruption investigation. We shall never get over that. I was glued to it all day. Got eye trouble. But there was Frank Costello—you know, a Cardinal Richelieu—Eminence Grise—distinguished wop—suddenly turned out to be just a kid off the block. Or Mayor O'Dwyer, soldier statesman—just another guy in a big hat.

PATRICK: And Hoover——

WEIDMAN: Noble as hell——

S. P: But surely Hoover was a great man—great organiser——

WEIDMAN: You should have heard him speak before Roosevelt was elected. That voice (*imitates a "beating of the wings of the angel of death" tone*) when he said: "If Franklin Roosevelt is elected, the grass will grow in a thousand cities, the homes of the people will fall open to the wind and to the rain."

S. P: How do you account for this corruption? (*Papers are full of it this week. Sixty police in mass trial. Moran, ex-fire-chief, rockily heroic in appearance, fined $2,000 and sent down for five years maximum.*)

WEIDMAN: It's not long since we were pushing westward over the Appalachians. There was still unclaimed land in Oklahoma in 1917. It's just the spirit of claiming new ground. It's the Battle of Agincourt —Greek landings at Pæstum——

S. P. (*taking off the top inch of a new martini in one gulp*): It's Exodus and Deuteronomy.

WEIDMAN: Deuteronomy isn't as good as that. Notice how we

---

say: "I can understand you perfectly well. It's the Park Avenue people I find difficult."

TAXI: And they're the ones who try to imitate English.

Roars of laughter all round. The taximan is just a Bronx voice straight out of a U.S. film in a Leicester Square cinema. Most of us have now lost and forgotten our first difficulty in understanding American talkies. This particular taxi-driver spoke with knowledge and eloquence about the loss of personal touch under our National Health Scheme.

shift from subject to subject? I can talk about anything. I'm oblivious to the next thing you're going to say. I——

PATRICK: That's a split infinitive——

S. P: Isn't it . . . a wrong use of . . .

WEIDMAN: And if *that* doesn't get them you can always quote them a statistic with a decimal point. When I was first in England they gave me a room in St. Martin's Lane with a neon light outside it. Neon! And I didn't even know they'd got electricity.

Oh, the difficulty of leaving people. It was now 8 o'clock and I had to be in black tie at the Paramounts for a "Ball"—she called it. Or was that at the Warfels? Rushed home and changed. Drove up to Paramounts late—they were leaving for us to dine at the Eddie Warfel's —famous banking family—six people.

I walked into the room without a trace of shyness to meet and talk quietly to these new friends, but instead I saw a picture. I looked again. There on the wall was a huge oil. A boy in faintly blue clothes— the image of Picasso's Blue Boy? Yet it couldn't possibly be Picasso's Blue Boy, because that sort of thing is reserved for the Hermitage or the Prado. Anyhow I mustn't stand too long staring. Better not to comment. Later they told me they were watching my reactions —it was, in fact, the original of Picasso's Blue Boy. As a sort of compromise, and to suggest I always stared at paintings, I carefully studied the rest of them, like a dog pretending to sniff the flower-bed after failing to catch a bird on the lawn. A Rouault and a Klee, pink patterns on a chocolate background . . . the Warfel champagne seemed to clear my head. One Klee was called "Romantic Party"; Klee had told Warfel it was meant to be "a Coney Island of objects you like to see and feel." I talked about how this hit the mood for a lot of people, and went on to say that letters of Rubens were full of good things like that. I felt under a personal obligation, as a European, to know more about some aspects of European painting than they did.

After cointreau we drove on to the Ball, also somewhere in the low Seventies latitude, with splendid forecourts and marble entrance halls. "Good," said Kodex, in our party, "they've shoo'd the cows away." Inside were glimpses of dignified social Americans talking calmly in fine evening dresses. "Very few sex maniacs *here*," says Kodex. "There's sometimes a very fine line . . ." I say. "Difficult to draw fine lines over enthusiasms," says Kodex, looking hard at a footman.

This dance turned out to be a fine bare-shouldered affair of high

Park Avenue quality. The women were very smart in a safe, introvert way. Nothing remotely suggesting an effort to follow a new Paris fashion. (One feels that the worst social floater would be to know, even by name, some stock glamour-woman from films, like Rita Hayworth.) This is a "dogwood" dance which means that the beautiful fat dogwood blossoms in sprays round the room thrust against the crowded heads of the dancers. I got rather bland again about this time, mentioning the dogwood. "It belongs to the *Ranunculaceæ* group," I said. People kept arguing about my future route, without taking much notice of me—on the best way to Go West, for instance. *Must* go through *Dallas*, Texas. No, Houston is *true* Texas. Do you want cowboys? *Must* stay with the Harmons, they have eight. The Huddlestones have bison which are practically wild. Jimmy Huddlestone really does come galloping up on a horse. He ought to see that.

I had been sitting out beside a rather attractive mature lady in black, with expensive but undertone jewellery. When she says "Don't you get bored with all the entertainment?" I try to look as if I were asked to dances like this every night and say, "To tell you the truth I rather like it." It seemed natural to me to touch her lightly on the wrist at this point and did. She stiffened for one moment, I thought. Did I do it wrong, or were wrists never lightningly touched in 72nd Street? "There is a slight difference of international custom here," I found myself saying. I should of course have said this to myself. Eddie W. saying, "What do you think of R. H. S. Crossman?" I found it difficult to switch so quickly to this celebrated left-winger. "Dick Crossman?" I say. "Wonderful man. Wonderful. Superb." However, I suddenly thought of the *New Statesman*. I was in no state to stick to my guns, so I added, "Frightful."

W: What?

S. P: Bad.

W: Crossman wrote that fine piece about the Middle East.

So he did, but I make up a name at random. "Oh, that was R. H. Tausix."

W: He's dead.

S. P: Well then, it must have been in the last three days. He was calling me from Washington the other day.

When my kind and charming dinner-hosts go, I leap up to go to Ed Condon's, where Ted is, to listen to connoisseur jazz.

That TV is Equally Casual

Friday, 11*th May*. America does *well* things like telephone messages when you are out. They are duplicated in legible writing and stamped with time of receipt. I feel sleepy and fuzzy after last night,[1] but I have to be at one of the fifty radio addresses for the Dorothy Dean TV show at 12.30. I had to discuss British and American humour with R. V., a famous middle-brow intellectual. On or off the screen, this tiny man never stopped talking and wisecracking in the inexhaustible American way till the end of the show. In the television studio they were setting a fashion parade which was to precede us. "A fight, that's what the audience want," R. V. said of our coming discussion. I was overcome by a feeling of fuzzy mildness. R. V. and I went out while I had a ham and cheese sandwich. I cashed travellers' cheques in the bank and R. V. kept saying to the bank manager, "Don't let him out of your sight"; to me he said, "I should settle for half if I were you." He is one of those sixty-ish men who take on the tone of a popular man whether he is popular or not.

Back in the television studio I feel hot. "Do I want make-up?" I want something to mop up the sweat. The models are practising their parade. The most attractive one has an even more beautiful face painted on top of her pretty features. She smiles first at a table with a pot of flowers on it, and then at me, both smiles with precisely the same intimate look of recognition, as she side-steps away from the camera in her fourth summer dress. She watches immobile while I, with a thin pancake almost immediately absorbed by my heat, am bundled into a tasteful wicker chair to be introduced, as if at some nightmare garden party, to the camera and the set.

"You all know Mr. Potter's wit and subtlety," says the hostess to a few hundred invisible viewers.

I smile uneasily, and am thunderstruck to spot a television screen in front of me where I see myself, though still I thought smiling, actually hollow-eyed, like a dead face looking up from the bottom of a pool. What are they saying? R .V., who does this sort of thing twice a week, is sailing into a witty attack on British humour. After a time I say something nice about the *New Yorker*, describing a drawing by Gluyas

[1] Note for counter-hangover specialists. Had this been London I should by this time have removed all traces of last night's excess by playing five games of squash in two sweaters. I mention this trivial fact because it is far from trivial to me, and the fact that it is somehow impossible here must disadvantageously affect other Englishmen too.

Williams. "Our humour is broader, stronger," says R. V., making no reply to my remark. "The rough vitality of the frontier." I wake up at this point and say quite brusquely that the Americans have pictures of themselves as tough frontiersmen whereas really they are rather diffident and introspective; while the English, though outwardly gentle, have cores of granite.

No one takes much notice of this and I feel the sweat on my back. How much longer to go? I glance at my wrist-watch. A little later a large notice is held up behind the camera: DO NOT LOOK AT WATCH. At the end our books are thrust into the jaws of the camera for a close-up: this is said to be good advertisement.

Two very young camera-men brought their *Lifemanship* to be autographed, so I (*a*) get back one point on tiny R. V., and (*b*) am confirmed in liking these long, pale, slack, graceful American boys.

That U.S. Hospitality is no Legend

Back to pack for Connecticut. Good to cross off Grand Central Station, where steam is a memory of old coaching days and where even trains are tucked away somewhere out of sight from these spacious courts. I get an evening paper the shape and weight of a Foreign Office brief-case.

In the train up north-west through White Plains and then into Connecticut. The country is leafy and English, with small spring trees, but the homes have not the over-cosy red bric-à-brac of their Woking English counterpart—the houses are white-boarded in a farmhouse style. At the station Raymond Massey came to meet me. The last time I saw Ray in the flesh was when he was a very young actor in London —Ackerley's wonderful play *Prisoners of War*. Now he has gone so far—he can get a fine big film part for the asking: and now because he had read my book and knew I was a stranger here, he was asking me, very properly, for the week-end.

Ray is a mixture of strength and gentleness—of Abraham Lincoln and a handsome Labrador dog, careful not to hurt anybody even when he wags his tail. His house is one of these clapper-boarded farmhouses; but inside it is not quite farmhouse. The floors are flooded with thick red carpet which pours out of the front door as you open it. A 1711 house has been cleverly enlarged, meticulously in the same style, including a fine and beamy barn, a splendid study for Ray. In a new small house adjoining live the Plymouth and the Cadillac and the chauffeur's own Ford (which would do so nicely for me) and the chauffeur and his wife. Two other staff, well-trained and invisible. Inside all is Third Empire—half serious, half parody. Third Empire cartoons and drawings on the walls—a pretty red in the carpets and curtains and silk-velvet hangings to the mantelpiece. And the comfort . . . in my guest-room, private bath and shower of course, but the variety of matching coloured towels in its bathroom . . . the perfect design of the breakfast tray, the dishes full of cigarettes, the pyramids of book-matches, the drinks always appearing, the milk, bananas, grapes and biscuits always renewed by my bedside, the flowers, the carefully chosen books . . . in my bathroom the extra rubber mat *in* the bath, to prevent slipping; the used razor-blade container in a matching colour.

It was very pretty; and Ray's original-beam study had Spy cartoons, files of *Country Life*, a fine bench round the fire carpentered by Ray himself, each of the eight supports carved with the initials of eight famous actresses who had played opposite him in his big parts.

Mrs. Massey I knew must be a born house-manager because she never seemed to be managing. She is of a different tempo from Ray and packs so many ideas into a minute of talk that I find myself talking simultaneously. A junior version of her prettiness is present—Dorothy's daughter, Dorothy II. Third member of party—Madie Christians, famous actress over here, amusing, quiet personality and, like every adult in this house, with deep ingrained knowledge of theatre—I thought of Athene Seyler.

This very exquisite Dorothy II, slender as a corn stem, was my introduction to American Youth. She is in her first year at Vassar. She is one of these U.S. girl phenomena. Very exact hair-do, reservedly nail-tinted, very fair skin with finest possible freckles, very smart, and —this is the fact for English county mothers to realise—sixteen; yet behaving grown up, without the slightest attempt to *make* herself older than she is. Is this cutting out of gawky adolescence the sign of a young nation? Does fourteen mean eighteen here, as it did with the Elizabethans or the Florentines? She is doing a general humanities course, majoring in drama. Keen to tell me all about Vassar. Smokes a little: drinks a little: and stays up a little for these very late endless talks we have. Describes how at Vassar all the girls wear jeans and scrubby hair-dos through the week (unless their boy-friend calls). Then on Friday they are all primped up to go home and "knock the Professor flat." I get from her some exactly contemporary words, some of them our own prep-school slang of twenty years ago. No longer is someone a HEEL, but a CREEP. Soft woolliness and feeble lack of charm is GREBY. The fluff left in your pockets is NERR. On the pond (duckweed and algæ) is SCHLURG. About Dorothy II there is no trace, no possible living speck, of creep, grebe, nerr or schlurg.[1]

It should have been a perfect week-end, and was, except that I *still* couldn't get my games exercise. I had to go more or less covertly on the wagon (this was a bit greby, although the Masseys never drink much themselves). Ray and I *did* play nine holes at the New Canaan golf-course, with a braw, ten-year-old, silent caddie with the longest black lashes I have ever seen. It is more or less automatic that even these minor golf-courses have hard tennis courts and a fine swimming-pool. They are often off-licence—"because of the teen-agers" (must write an article on Teenocracy). I did go for a forty-minute walk, thoro' bush thoro' briar, by myself, early on Sunday morning, before they were up, and came back dusty to find them all waiting for me in a new set, inspired by Saturday's conception of open air, of country clothes.

This evening we sat round, talking. "We always talk to all hours," and a lot of the time simultaneously. "Stephen won't want to hear about that" . . . "Do let me speak for a moment." (I was talking fairly continuously as well.) Manhattans always to hand. I secretly poured one or two of mine into a plant-pot in the corner. This plant earth soon began to smell slightly of whisky; but only the big Alsatian seemed to notice. With extraordinary kindness, knowledge, and helpfulness, the Masseys advised me about the TV rights of *Gamesmanship*. They really know the subject from both ends—of art and business. Dorothy would say: "But I'm not going to have that Mr. What-is-it of yours saying a guaranteed fifteen minutes—I don't like the sound of it." Ray: "Now don't, Dorothy, you've said all that before." "That little feller——" "Look, may I speak——" "If you can. I'm waiting. Look, Stephen, it's not people like us that have television sets, it's the small farmers, washers-up—now I've never washed-up in my life."

Dog sniffs flower-pot. Looks questioningly at Dorothy.

Ray: "Bosh, Dorothy, can I say something here——" "Toodles must wait" (because she has placed a piece of candy on the paw of

---

[1] Typical Anglo-American situation. I, coming from the country of classic English where exact derivational meanings are lovingly preserved, am particularly fond of U.S. invented slang, or U.S. neologisms.

Toodles the dog. His tail lashes the floor while Third Empire china shudders and shakes). "Paid for!"

The Alsatian takes no notice, goes on thundering on the carpet. An ash-tray slips to the floor.

"Now let's try Henry Brice. Dot dear" (to daughter), "find Station Seven. Stephen, you ought to learn our television. Now this is Henry Brice's production."

This, my first sight of U.S. TV, was a conventional, ill-produced, unimaginative "stock" view of horrors in Korea.

"Bad. Now let's try Uppie Peppingham—just the man to compère your television." On Station Five a funny Uppie Peppingham programme was starting. To my surprise and pleased interest this turned out to be a parody of a B.B.C. television quiz. The American Stage Englishman and the American Stage Cockney were both exemplified, plus a "refined" announcer. This wasn't much good either, and the Masseys were apologetic. But all American wit, even Benchley's or Thurber's, seems to go coarse on them when they satirise the English. It is not second-hand but hundredth-hand, twenty years out of date and based entirely on stock "national caricature" figures. If only they knew how much funnier, more absurd and more harshly caricaturable we are in real life. The Masseys were embarrassed by this harmless stuff. "Quite all right," I said, Englishly, and continued truthfully: "The English satirising Americans are just as bad. And there is *one* American who can imitate Englishness to perfection—Danny Kaye." We changed to Channel Three, which was all-in wrestling. These "wrestlers" seem to be trained tumblers, going through long-practised routines, which mostly consist in throwing a big man on his fat-padded back so that he bounces. They pretend to break rules, and the referee pretends to disqualify them. The crowd of mild Babbitts pretends to be angry, appreciative, excited and brutalised.

Dorothy II tells me that this Schnabel (on the screen) is the most hated wrestler. Bad loser, she says. So was Beethoven, I say. "But only from 1804 to 1812," says Dorothy II, knowing more about this subject than I do. Madie Christians starts talking about music. The big dog, taking one last fascinated sniff at the flower-pot, gives me a once-over lick in an excess of admiring love. Thump goes the TV set as Beethoven hits the boards. Dorothy I says: "Stephen, don't you think the Americans are less inhibited than the British?" I do not really think so; but I think they are less inhibited in their hospitality: and I shall remember this first experience of it.

Of course this special hospitality (which I call in my own mind Creative Greeting hospitality) is a famous national characteristic. Now that I am going again, I find myself looking forward to more than one kind of warmth. Is there a cause for it? "Kindness" doesn't do justice to a certain alert and appreciative curiosity. Maybe certain southern States are as cagey as some northern English counties, and the villains of the comic strips invariably have Asiatic cheekbones; maybe the American citizen can work off the primitive dislike of furriners against neighbours and rival States; maybe the attraction which this most passionately nationalistic nation finds in Europeans is partly umbilical; but whatever the cause, the savour of the U.S. welcome is the best in the world. They not only want to know you, they actually want to show you as well, to be guides. One needs a tin-opener, perhaps used in combination with a corkscrew, to find out from an Englishman what local custom, beauty, or celebrated historical association it is he most values in his own county. The Americans are different.

This made my "crossing off" tour easier and pleasanter than I thought possible, though it made me also want to do too much. One more quotation from 1951 (Boston):

My taxi-driver didn't think much of Boston. I spoke of Connecticut. "Ah, that's the most modern State in the Union," he said. "Most go-ahead." What is Boston in a word? "Dull," he said. "Out of date. Go-slow." Presumably, for true Bostonians, that is the delightful point of it, and as that is what I had always heard, even from my genuine Bostonian friend Evarts, so un-American in accent that prolonged microscopic examination of his speech will reveal a slight un-Englishness in his pronunciation of two words only—"moostache" and "glaycier." I just had time to see the big obelisk for Bunker's Hill (where one understands the British made some sort of strategic retreat) before being lulled into gentle streets and charming houses which were like a fresh manifestation of Englishness rather than a new sight of the United States. The paint on Charles Morton's fence is patchy and worn, but big bushes of lilac and wistaria hide it. All is small with sun. More exactly English is the house of Murray Forbes, where the main living-room is a sort of small panelled college-hall with a minstrel's gallery (1780) and a grand piano which of course I immediately start playing, noting that (whereas in England my playing is angrily disregarded) the children, including one aged four and wearing a large button with "4" on it as proof, are told to keep quiet when I start. Next day I was shown the "Bullfinch" houses; Bullfinch is the great New England architect of *c.* 1820—Regency houses with Regency ironwork, bow fronts and cornices, but with the pleasing variation of dull red brick instead of stucco. In genuine Bullfinches the window glass has gone violet with age. In the thirties imitation violet was sometimes put in; now even the imitation violet is sought after, and there is a trade (perhaps) in imitating imitation "thirties" violet. Louisburg Square, in atmosphere, is very like a Brighton square. I am taken into a pretty Georgian room—Jenny Lind was married from it in 1852. On Christmas Eve candles are put in all the Square windows and anybody can go in. I am sure that's not quite so English as I would like to think it is.

After Boston (I can see now) the speed of this journey got rather out of control. No time for a diary. I had the feeling that I must see as many landmarks as possible in case I never came again. Still more, in case I did come again. A first quick all-over taking-in of the whole thing has always been the best way, for me, of starting a new subject. It makes it easier, next time, to see an inch beneath the surface.

In Washington I remember realising that the great Washington monuments, of which it is no bad thing in Washington to feign ignorance (I asked J. Bryan to meet me "by the Harding Memorial"), were built in an age before the U.S. found its own architectural and sculptural style, but although they are traditional and even conventional in design, their placing (especially the Jefferson) and the conviction and pride with which they were constructed and are enjoyed, make them good in a way which photographs can never explain.

It was in Georgia airport that I first experienced the shock, so fascinating to a European and cue for such endless powerful letters in English newspapers from addresses like The Old Rectory, Westchurch-on-the-Ooze, where the problem of segregation is a shade less immediate and concrete, that white men went into one lavatory and negroes into another. I think the shock is something to do with the sudden opposition between a subjective Darwinian conviction that we are all the same race and an equally irrefutable objective demonstration that we are not. No doubt Swift would have been very strong on this subject, and would have invented a new Laputa to explain how one breed of dogs was confined to lamp-posts on the left side of the street, another on the right; and indeed one's first reaction is to smile tolerantly. But it is only distance which makes the problem seem small. Close to, one feels frightened by its size, and becomes Gulliver not in Lilliput but in Brobdingnag.

In New Orleans I was made to comprehend the ancientness of Jazz by the age of the grizzled old masterpieces who played Dixieland piano-music so brilliantly in the bars of the Vieux Carrée. I was realising also the fact that this kind of latitude is hotter, since my farthest south hitherto had been Bethlehem. My chief memory of my next stop on that latitude, Dallas, Texas, was the unpopularity of the spontaneous gesture when I opened the anti-insect wire door of my hostess's kitchen to step out under the blinding stars and came back to find her fighting with flying roaches the size and weight of squash-balls.

In Dallas an open car full of check-shirted Texans stopped dead in the street when they saw me and said, "Why, he's an Englishman." Next day, on my way to Los Angeles, I tried, as a kind of exercise, to explain to an Irish air hostess, a hotel man from Miami, and a Scripps Howard journalist from Maine, that I was the only man in the aircraft without an accent. Gary Cooper was also there. It was interesting to confirm that the leisurely and charming personality he expresses in his films is a re-created version of his own. I also noted that he looks much younger than he has appeared in recent films. The camera seems to work on the skin like a plough.

Every American told me that Los Angeles was too vague and sprawling to be a place, so sprawling is how I saw it. My business excuse to be there was a meeting with Cary Grant, who is Games-manship-minded: he also bears a striking resemblance to his film personality; though, again, he is younger and better-looking. He took me round the Twentieth Century lot, a state of twenty townlets all in different periods, of different nations, Nineveh B.C., Carcasonne A.D., or Two Springs, North Dakota. And every street of every city had fronts but no backs, like an eigh-teenth-century folly imagined by an American millionaire.

Familiar film sight—in fact some of these ancient palaces were genuinely ageing, and holes were showing through mock ruins in the wrong places. The surprise was to see that the private houses of the stars of the film colony belonged to the same style. Each house different, of course—each a different specimen, a turret of Château d'If, a fifteenth-century cottage out of Laven-ham, a Normandy fisherman's cliff hut, all made out of the same concrete or plaster mixture.

A car is essential in Los Angeles, so as Grant had a new Cadillac to spare he naturally (it's natural in U.S.) prepared to hand it over to me for my stay. I badly wanted to use it to call on a beautiful film star, Angela Lansbury, with whom I wanted to clinch a declaration of love made to me at the time of her resi-dence in Weymouth Avenue, Mill Hill, London, not long ago when she was six years old. But so instantly did this Cadillac, this thoroughbred of silent and resilient speed, recognise my unworthiness as a rider that for the first and last time in its life it refused to move and all the pushing of all the carpenters and plasterers of Twentieth Century Fox failed to make it.[1]

Santa Barbara–San Francisco. I was "doing" America in so much more American a way than the Americans are said to "do"

[1] Note for serious games players. In California I realised that games instruction is not dependent on a few men who happen to be able to teach. In the U.S. teaching is so organised and so frameworked with standardised basic principles, all stemming from a few great teachers, that even the pro at the small hotel can give you good and lasting benefit. The hospitality grapevine failed in Hollywood so that I had to live at the large Beverly Hills Hotel, my most expensive to date: but worth it, because in one hour's lawn tennis lesson from the Beverly teacher I learnt more than from all the lessons I have ever had in England.

Europe—for me the appetite for this kind of travel grows with what it feeds on. The slight loneliness, minor discomforts and featherweight disasters are absorbed in and counteracted by a huge superficial satisfaction.

I am looking forward even more to this return, not only because this time I've got the right companion, but also because in 1951 there was that small shadow, and now that is passing. The shadow of McCarthy was big in 1951. It seemed from this side of the Atlantic that America had gone most un-Americanly mad in an attack on what was topsy-turvily called un-Americanism. All this was not something even the unpolitical-minded could pettishly ignore, in the English Heartbreak House style. The confusing part of it was that the basis of McCarthyism, a word suggestive of all bad emotions, was a rational one. There is a perfectly good case for not giving freedom to a way of life (Communism) which is opposed to freedom. It is at least arguable that freedom must be worked for, not just taken for granted. Yet the dangers of making even this particular exception to the laws of freedom were being classically demonstrated. For every ten Lincoln-minded men in the United States, there is one sprat of a Louisiana Kingfish; and it is these demagogues who by their nature get the publicity, particularly the publicity abroad.

They get it to such an extent that in 1951 Europeans were taking the small rotten part for the otherwise sound whole. Demagoguery breeds demagoguery: and behold over here we had the distasteful sight of naturally liberal-minded people being illiberal about a defection from liberal grace. I have a biggish block of English friends who in the twenties stood up nobly for the Left against a rigid, domineering, and sometimes cruel Right. The rigid Right having been (partly through their efforts) very properly put under more decent control in the thirties and forties, these fighting liberals, left dangling in the air or no longer active, were chafing for something to hit at. America was a heaven-sent target. The best of them fastened on McCarthyism's worst aspect—the "screening" of creative artists,

and the discrimination against writers in Hollywood and elsewhere who refused to say the right thing at the right moment.
The rest of us felt sore with America, and sore with our friends
at the same time; and that was the worst of it—this making a sore
place.

When I was in the States things began to look rather different.
No doubt this was partly because the kind of politicians connected
with McCarthy couldn't have possibly come within a brassie-
shot of any of the Americans I was likely to meet. I also found
that in the eloquence and trenchancy of their own vilification
of McCarthyism the Americans went far further in their self-
criticism than the most caustic European commentator. The
remorseless anti-McCarthy cartoons of Herblock of the *Washington Post* made David Low seem tea-party by comparison.

It was for the Americans to heal their own sores—yet still the
advice and criticism from England poured out. Among the weekly
papers in the New York clubs, the most difficult one not to read
is the one with the leading article printed on the first page—
our own excellent, well-edited, and pungent *New Statesman*.
Every week at this time, page one was the anti-American article.
The American warmongers. American hysteria. No doubt some
of these accusations may have been true as criticisms of government policy. But the fact is that almost every single man who
momentarily waxed grim or looked humorously quizzical as he
glanced at his own condemnation had some relation who was
fighting in Korea, possibly even a son killed in that dreary and
dusty peninsula—some friend, at any rate, who had gone there,
as my own son had gone, believing that by this act he was
doing something for world peace, something against a war-
making Communism. Of course to most Londoners the first
few pages of the *New Statesman* are at worst just dear old
Kingsley doing one of his griefs in a crown of thorns from
Clarkson's, to quote the unfair old joke—taking a line and being
a good Fleet Street editor. But in these pleasantly hospitable
clubs I was strongly inclined to bury the *New Statesman* out of

sight. I longed for a dummy Page One to stick on the front. Liberals were dismayed because these views proved the brazen "pink" tendencies and impertinence of Great Britain to delighted isolationists. A week or so later K. M. printed a "confession" from "captured American airmen." Full details of germ warfare. At best it only added to the gloom—and to the support of the new Ism, now that McCarthy was waning, of MacArthur, whose recorded voice was heard repeating endlessly, in Macy's store, for a solid week, the MacArthur resignation speech. It all cast a cloud, not least because of the feeling that someone or other, and more than one someone, was with the best intentions preparing for himself the special purgatory reserved for those who help to set England and America at odds.

*   *   *   *   *

Well, now thank goodness that particular shadow is dwindling. And back on the solid British deck of the S.S. *Tweedledum*—which reminds me that I ought to be *keenly observing*. Commissioned radio, commissioned articles about this trip are the money for First Class, and indeed the financially essential point of it. But I feel vague, if not tired. We had to get up at 6.30. Being a man, I take half an hour longer to come awake than H. I am wool, but she, thank goodness, is scissors. Yet I had prepared everything— not only position of passport: I had even rehearsed keeping biro in left pocket, for instance, and small magnifying glass in inner right. I seemed to have plenty of time, until, one thing to go wrong, 7.30 turned out to be 7.55. My watch had stopped. I had to rush the bags down, H. helping, chipping off wallpaper from our narrow staircase. I sat in the taxi in a sweat while H.'s hand, holding mine, was as cool as a slice of tongue, not a hair of her head out of place, her appearance exactly perfect. To me it always seems that such incidents are malicious bad luck.

In the boat-train a small thing happened differently from the way I wanted it. Though apparently looking calmly straight ahead, her hair done in a new and immaculate shape, with a little green hat on the back of it, which she had coolly taken a quarter of an hour to put on even on this great day of exodus, H. was sizing up our fellow-travellers, and making use of her power to overhear conversations five small breakfast tables away. The weather spell was still getting a few last cuts at us—shoals of snow outside the window, snow lying as fresh as if it were the first instead of the last day of winter on the roofs and hedges, new snow emphasising the shabbiness and pointlessness, the potty backyard effect of the houses lined up below the embankment. A big American with a fine big suit, uncreased as armour, and fine flashing mouth, was talking at large. "We'd have pulled all this down long ago . . . you should see what they're doing in Western Germany . . . England's right behind in building . . . where's your new housing schemes? Look at Sweden. Look at Brazil." The Englishman he was talking to looked polite and unhappy.

"Even his teeth are new," said H., still looking straight ahead. "I know," I said. A wrong start, but fatal for me to assume a great understanding voice at that moment and say that Americans aren't really like that, although a few of them behave like caricatures of themselves when they are abroad, and so do we, and so on, because I am not going to try to sell America to H. Either she likes it or not.

Fellow-passengers looked at each other distastefully at the barrier—this was our first sight of ourselves. The *Tweedledum* was round the corner.

"It's not very big," said H. We could only see the bows. The bows looked almost mean. Where is your "lean and lithe like a greyhound"? Perhaps bows are a little too small and body a little too fat, a mixture of bulldog body and collie nose. But now there was this wall of some great Ministry of Information building above us. Only the gangway entrance to remind us it is a ship. Mannerly greetings from stewards. H. started to unpack while I went to the sun-deck.

And now, as I stare down into that dead water, the gap starts to widen. With neither sound nor effort, we are beginning to slide, like a glacier. The woman beside me is waving faster, but her waving tails away, and she allows herself to look miserable, now that her face is far enough away. A group of quayside-wavers in the space reserved, I expect, for Tourist-class good-byes, are singing "D'ye ken John Peel," and it's getting fainter. Yorkshire people, I expect. "Yes, I ken John Peel and Ruby too, Ranter and Ringworm and Dry-rot too," or whatever it is. How glad I am to get away from it. I'm sick of things I normally love—of old English songs, of picturesque spots, of typical English spinsters at Seaford, of words like Bovril or Hovis written up, which I've been seeing since before I was able to read, of feeling I ought to study what Who says about It in the *Observer*, of celebrated little hedgerow flowers coming up according to weekly schedule. Of course the yellow of the tentative coltsfoot on the embankment between the snow patches was touching, but I am longing for something less diffident and am sick of the general tameness of the wild life on my particular beat. I am sick of the way London goes on repeating itself diminuendo and deadendo through the dreary ways out of it, so that you can't get clear of it; of grimly sexy little shops in Tottenham Court Road, of old oldness, of used-up worn-ness, of the Kensington-ness of Stagnant Gardens, S.W.3; of the worth and rightness of *The Times* and the B.B.C., of the dusty sparrows round the boundary of Lord's, of the keep-offness, don't-touchness of the Ancient Flints department of the British Museum, or Hyde Park. Hyde Park . . . Central Park. One touch of Central Park, and the idea of "Park" will come to life again. Give the concept of "Park" that quarter-turn, and the whole thing clicks into focus once more: and Hyde Park will freshen again in my mind's eye, and I shall want to see it again. "When you see Central Park . . ." I think of beginning, to H.

But I'm not going to say anything about this now. I hear that American booming again. H. likes the quick, crisp, com-pressed-mouth American voice, like Joe's. "It's only the slow, deep confident voice that gets me," she says. I'm not going to tell her that I quite like it for a change, or point out that it's the opposite quality in the English voice which Americans dislike, the English habit of speaking in echoless, matt voices, from the front of the face only, dropping syllables out like bits of gum with the taste sucked out of them. All this reminds me, while I am taking a last look at the ship as ship and not yet floating Tudor Cocktail Lounge, that it wouldn't be a bad idea if I were to deepen up my voice a bit, slow it up, and stop my occasional habit of walking absent-mindedly up and down patting the back of my head. Americans don't like it, and there's no point in putting them off unnecessarily.

Marvel at the casualness of the departure of these large liners. There is no visible signal, still less a shout, passing between ship and shore, ship and tug. There is one sailor in the rigging—but he is looking the other way. Two officers on the bridge, but their thoughts seem far off, as two tugs steam full speed ahead at our bows. The captain of one tug, while his prow is recklessly charging into ours, turns his back on the whole scene and reads a newspaper. The only sound-effect is the famous one of gulls. The black-headed really have black heads—hopeful sign of summer.

In our cabin H., with her knowledge of yachts and small liners in the Red Sea, is going to teach me how to be shipshape and tidy, how to put everything in a certain place and keep it there. This I am determined to do. When I said five weeks ago, "I shall have to go to the U.S.—you will come too?" she had already, before I got to the word "too," discarded five suits in favour of six she had decided on as being more suitable for A Deck. Her small beauty-box was twice as heavy as usual—I know she thinks of it as an armoury against a strange and hostile race.

Though we are in the cheapest cabin available, it is First Class, and we are people of privilege. The old passenger hands bury themselves during these preliminary hours. There are even some transatlantic sophisticates who never appear till the third day. We, new to it, are gazing respectfully at the loftiness of the

34

restaurant, and the depths of the swimming-pool. On the Hammond organ Mr. Watkins Tyler is playing "Violets in a Surrey Garden." "Some sort of sea-shanty, I suppose," H. says.

For ten minutes we walk without seeing one object suggestive of a ship or shipboard, except for a bas-relief of dolphins in shiny walnut. Impossible to tell which is fore, which aft. "Which way round are we?" woman in orchid asks steward. A lot of them have big floppy orchids. "There is a diagram by the main deck on each staircase, Madam," he says. "You'll be quite a sailor in a day or two."

"Land on the starboard bow," I say; which means nothing more than that I have caught sight of the dwindling Portlington crematorium between the legs of a bronze Statue Group of three thin boys holding up a plateful of swordfish.

"It's certainly comfortable," H. says. So comfortable that soon we shall feel as if even our bones are softening. But H. is frowning at the parallelograms on the chintzes, the rust-and-sky-blue patterns on the carpets. "What is the period?" It is full of sharp angles, stylised fauns, conventionalised centaurs, simplified birds, and generalised pomegranates.

I give H. one of my lectures. If you want to give it a name you might say "Directress 1933." That is to say that it contains the safest and worst elements of a vogue (unrealistic cubist cocktail) already in 1933 (because *Tweedledum* was so far behind schedule) five years out of date. The style chosen by the wives of the directors. Some of the worst effects in Company Decoration are due to Directress influence. But perhaps, after all, in this case the wives were advanced. There was too much up-to-date-ness about it, so that it has never been anything but out of date

Yet I really enjoy the decoration. The undertaking was an effort, and therefore a something, certainly with a one-pieceness about it, and therefore giving interest if not æsthetic pleasure. It was bold to commission Edward Wadsworth (I remember him making studies—more like diagrams—for his pier-and-shells mural, at Maresfield, as precise and exact as a watchmaker). I think, then, we thought the décor, and the choice of artists, an advanced step. Anyhow it is all good solid stuff, meant to last, and brings solid British worth right into the jaws of the Hudson River, ramming it into the gums of Quay Ninety, West Side, Manhattan.

10th–14th March. England to New York. I expect that the thousand-odd crew know the life-cycle of the Atlantic Passenger, and could tell a Day One-er from a Day Three-er at a glance. Early stages include an aloof stage, and a determination-to-take-the-opportunity-to-do-some-useful-work stage.

We notice, by Day Three, that it is possible not only to look at but to see the ocean: our eyes relax, and we stare over the side. It is calm. The prow of the ship slits the sea surface like a dress. There is endless fracturing and re-fracturing of water-foam to stare at. The staring times get longer; deciding things takes longer, as we adjust to time-tables like:

10 a.m. Observation Competition. How many names in passenger list contain the word "Cat"?

11 a.m. The Audrey Plimm Fantaisie Quintette.

2.40 p.m. Enter for ping-pong competition.

3.50 p.m. Kindly attend "Clearance Officer" in Lounge.

What nonsense to say "what nonsense". The *Dum* understands us better than we do ourselves. Soon it is only by concentrated parcelling of time that we can make "ping-pong: 2.40" without a scramble.

Towards evening of Day Two there was a general disappearance. From tonight all change for dinner. Women have been assuming the impersonal look, the unseeing, don't-touch-me look they have when they are about to dress for a party.

Not H. She has such years of dressing up behind her that she puts on her face and her flame Balanciaga with fingers as smooth and effective as an old groom's when he saddles a horse. Ready before I am, she sits reading my *History of White's Club* (which

I have brought to work on my article on London Clubs for Ted Patrick) while her nail-varnish dries.

Tentative, Day Two dresses are not very deep and on the short side. H., sensing this, has decided on long, alone is long. She talks again of having some of her evening dresses cut short. "Long suits long women—that is the point," I say. H. is tall.

"One might as well be still wearing crinolines," H. says, "according to you; or woad." People at dinner talk, but nobody listens to anybody; their eyes are wandering over everybody else.

A few "characters" begin to emerge. A spare, tidy, clipped-all-over man, who does an hour's timed and measured walking on the sun-deck twice a day. We call him Stomper. The fact that he is walking nowhere produces a look of special purpose-fulness. Another deck-walker has a kind of loose, metal shoe-heel which clinks him into sight and out again, his wife following with a loosely weaving walk, trying to keep up. Clinker always overhauls Stomper.

There is a tiny round man like one of those toys weighted in the lower half you can't knock over. Nottingham business-man perhaps, doing a bust by taking his wife, and finding it no spree at all because nobody talks to them, nobody says good morning, and his baby face looks defiant in consequence. H. talks of him as "sweet," as if he were a peke; and he is much cheered up when she says "Good morning."

There is the lady all alone at her table who has made no contacts yet but is sharpening up her sociability and giving neighbours a preview of her powers by using a deep fascinating voice when talking to her table-steward and, without for a moment losing her sense of position, flirting with him. He responds mechanically, having met it fifty times before.

Is it the influence of H. which makes such foibles in men seem rather lovable, not so in women? Her theory is that boys are more absorbed and unself-conscious than girls, and that this trait and difference are maintained in the grown-up state. When I am about to set off from the club-house for an important golf match at Rye, it is wonderful to have her with me to watch, but she will say, "Have you got your little bucket?"

It's just warm enough to sit on the sun-deck. Under our noses the deck-hand tarring the rope is pale—on modern ships the jolly tar spends most of his life underground. They have a tiny piece of sun-deck for spare moments, "but all the spare moments are gone by the time it takes to get there," they told me. Pale, but he looks very tough to me. I feel idiotic when under his nose the deck-steward lifts my feet up to wrap them in a blanket. No sign of scorn, however, from the tarring sailor, no notice whatever. H. (never the slightest degree ashamed of being comfortable) watches the sailor. "Look at him in his little black tam-o'-shanter—it's just like James," she says (James is ten), "up one side—down the other—and he whistles as he sticks the brush in the pot, and stops and presses his lips together as he starts the brush-stroke—just like James."

Half-way over and dead calm; but with food always stacked at the elbow, stomachs are feeling the strain. I put mine nearly right by walking eight miles round the deck, part of it before breakfast, and irritatedly banging into Stomper and Clinker at the corners. America approaching now, and as before it makes me have daydreams. . . . It is Washington, D.C., and a letter is waiting for me at the Hay Addams Hotel. *But how did anybody know I was going to stay there? What's it all about?* "A group of five of us, all admirers of yours . . . don't let it put you off when we say that two of us are from the Pentagon, two in the State Department. . . ." Suddenly I am in that mysterious little annexe to the White House. Two armed guards call me "sir." A brilliantly smart female secretary asks me about my work on Coleridge. "How exciting it must have been to find that letter to Thomas Poole in the British Museum. Tell me about it," she says. Outside the cherry trees are covered with pink sauce. But it is lifemanship they want. All stand up as I come in. "If, somehow, this whole neurosis which is shattering the Western peoples could be reduced by the solvent of your deliciously light touch. . . ." The suggestion came from a very high quarter indeed. It is inevitable—High Quarter and I talk it all out on Burning Tree Golf Course. "If it worked, Mr. Potter, I say *if* it worked (how surprisingly strong his accent was), there is always the possibility, for you, of the Chair of Social Behaviour at Yale. You would be required, of course, to deliver one lecture a year. . . ." "We're not certain, yet." This was a man with enormous eyebrows, who hitherto had not spoken. "We can't be certain that this means the end of international misunderstanding for ever. But if it does. . . ."

I am called back to consciousness by a tremendous scowling and yowling from the dog-kennels by No. 14 boat-station. They want breakfast.

Only three people at 8.15 a.m. in the big restaurant, and forty waiters. H. still asleep. Talk to our waiter—neat, pale, tender, quick (he clashes a lighter in H.'s face almost before she has put her cigarette in her mouth). He rolls up a trolley now with a dozen different kinds of honey, jelly, and marmalade—at my elbow almost before I know I want it. I wonder why he must carve and sharpen his little head smaller with a crew cut. Some of the younger members of these English crews get half Americanised.

"And you have sixteen hours then, in New York?" I say. "What do you do?"

"Well, I always listen to jazz."

"What, at a dance hall?"

"No—Birdland. It's quite good. Any time between ten at night and four in the morning. You just go and listen. Oh yes, you get Jo Kolony and Blinkers Red."

He's a member of the Park Street Rhythm Club, Southampton. A highbrow of this art, he is quietly interested in the dance-life of his state-room passengers who are prepared to jig round with perfect complacency to the oom-cha-cha, oom-cha-cha of the Audrey Plimm Quintette. Incident after breakfast. I was knocked out of the second round of the ping-pong tournament.

Today all thoughts of keeping ourselves to ourselves are melted, and we find ourselves eagerly having drinks before lunch with the Gollanczes, in front of a Zinkeisenish mural of a masked ball. We get through a whole tray of cocktail food while I discuss, in a storm of chat pent up for two days, such mutual friends as Francis, Joad, Farjeon, Gollancz enthusiastically chumping cheese biscuits while he talks and cascading crumbs over H., who much enjoys his eloquence, and it is refreshing to get V. G.'s penetrating comments on these friends of twenty-five years ago. After three and a half days it seems O.K. to chat to one or two of the people reclining in two blankets beside us on the sun-deck. H., reading at the speed of Macaulay, finishes *Honours for Sale*, six seconds a page, and starts *The Devils of Loudoun* (eight seconds). More breaking down of barriers under the benign influence of six o'clock. We play bridge with the Gollanczes till two. While H. and pretty Mrs. Gollancz remain calm, reasonable, well-pressed, and good-tempered, V. G. and I get more and more ruffled, show more signs of wear, with the deep untidiness and general rot bridge brings to men. H., even at 2 a.m., is impeccable and clear; G. and I are submerged under crumples and ash. Mrs. G., a beginner, makes large, mild, poised mistakes; G. stops everything dead and explains how she went wrong—all this without the slightest recrimination. In a pause, while we are having drinks and sandwiches, he talks about one of his recent publications, *Yield to the Night*—Joan Henry's book on a woman in a death-cell—and he tells how the thought of hanging always made him feel uncomfortable and sick since he was a boy, as if this feeling was peculiar and particular to him. "Since I was a child I never sleep on the night of an execution, if I know there is going to be one." I think in some others this would justify a charge of what I call spiritual swank, but in V. G. it is not, and after all, he has the right to speak of such things, having taken the trouble to do something to alter them.

When he asks me what I am writing he doesn't wait for an

answer but says, "I am doing a huge anthology of the human spirit, about four hundred pages. I don't think there has ever been anything like it." He asked me to suggest some pertinent prose passages from Coleridge, the only English writer, besides Blake, truly eloquent on this theme. I was glad I still remembered some of the direction posts to the inspired muddle of Coleridge. To straighten myself out from bridge collapse, I suggest to H. that we dance a little in the Starlight Room. The tempo of the fox-trot belonged to the slinky-slow period, dated precisely to the very month when *Tweedledum's* keel was laid.

Although we get an extra hour every day as we approach New York, the press of totally unimportant events bears so heavily on us that we always seem to be late up and behind time. I am making H. do a good deal of preparatory work on New York guide-books. I always believe the more you do beforehand the better. She realises now that Manhattan is pear-shaped, because I explain this to her every evening. I draw a lot of street-patterns, and she reads guides till she says she is beginning to know less than when she started.

Monday, 14th March. We got to New York today at the perfect time—i.e. dusk. The first sight of American land by this route could not be less dramatic in spite of the thrilling name Nantucket. Long Island is all longness and lowness, and H. took a good deal of digging up from below decks to come and look at it, she being fifty times more voyage-hardened than I am. Then of course, as we stopped for the pilot, the estuary became more interesting and the south end of Manhattan was visible as a low crop of fungus-stalks, peculiar but not yet translatable into any-thing perturbing or wondrous.

But twenty minutes later arrived the most exciting sight of either of our lives. When I came up again I found that the whole ship had returned to its primeval classlessness. Tourist, Cabin and First were all forward together, all staring, silent. Mixed in with our glum little Nottingham businessmen of the First Class and their tiny round wives were gracious Slavs and noble Greek immigrants with long raven hair seeing their new home for the first time. The promised land was worthy of the occasion, because as day began to melt into night, drove by drove the lights came on. Everything changed from an aloofness of vast shapes into something near, delicate, and exact, like a doll's-house or a model at a fair, for children: but superb. All the faces were solemn, all held in the same slow gaze. A little French child, with a child's gift of not looking where it was supposed to be looking, kept calling to his mother to admire a sailor climbing the rigging just in front of his face. "Regardez le matelot . . . regardez, regardez le matelot en haut, sur le grand mât." Otherwise silence.

Getting our bags to the hotel I only did one wrong thing. For some reason I was nagged by the thought of the novice-traveller, "Don't be had—don't overtip"; and when a freelance coloured porter moved our bags and helped us cram them into the taxi, I gave him a quarter (2s.). He was young and delicate. "Have a heart," he said, with a soft, feminine, cultured kind of raillery. He was pitch-black. "The poor must live," he said. It was the intonation of Max Beerbohm.

Later that night I walked H. from the Gladstone to Times Square, so excited that I overdid my running commentary. "You needn't actually say 'gramophone shop' when we see a gramophone shop," she said. She loved New York from that first walk, and will, I should say, for ever.

15th–18th March. New York—but my notes are too brief and my memory rather vague. I was enjoying seeing H. enjoying it and looking at it, and rather forgot to look intelligently myself. I also wanted to introduce H. to my friends. What do the Americans think of English women—and vice versa? *Item:* the English believe American women all start as Marilyn Monroes, and then with desperate rapidity change to Helen Hokinson types, all trace of figure and complexion gone for ever. (Personally, I see few signs of either extremes in New York City.) *Item:* the Americans believe English women to be thick, tweedy, and shire-bred. In other words, both sides generalise from one arbitrarily chosen type. (It seems to most travelled Londoners that they see more beautiful women in London than in any other city: New Yorkers feel the same about New York. No doubt local custom, national taste, and knowing where to look play a large part here.) To come to the point, whatever the American preconceptions of our women may be, H. is not thick and tweedy. One morning, for instance, she went to the New York Public Library to look up some facts for her new book, before joining two editors, who had by no means met her, and myself for lunch at the Algonquin. I told them my wife would be late because she was up to her elbows in research in the ancient manuscripts room, suggesting that when she was really on the trail she lost all sense of time and wore, as it were, the same tartan jeans for months together. H. came at last—in a suit as well-turned and limber as her head.

Tuesday, 15th March. We cash our travellers' cheques at the bank on Madison. Every time I go there to the money-changing department, the junior man is getting on the nerves of his senior and there is about to be an explosion which never comes. The junior is older—a small man with bulging eyes and flat grey hair, who never changes his expression or the speed of his intentionally over-deliberate movement. "Can you deal with this then, Mr. Hickleback?" the senior man says without looking up, deeply angry. Junior turns towards me slowly as if he was standing on a turn-table. The same thing happens every time, and the explosion still remains just below ignition-point ever since 1951.

At Holt's, U.S. publisher of *Gamesmanship*, I see Bill Buckley. Bill starts the Holt hospitality going by offering to get us tickets for the most packed-out and unapproachable theatre in New York (*The Pajama Game*). He rings up some man-of-mystery middleman. He says, "Those tickets you gave me last week were in Row Q—practically outside the theatre. Look, I don't want to upset your pregnancy over this, but you must do better." Bill says the new play at the Winter Garden is a "nervous hit."

On the seat of the hotel lift at 6 o'clock in the evening is next

43

day's *Mirror*, weighing half a pound, and at least three and a half ounces of it all about the Jelke case. Reading this kind of paper one gets the feeling that stately old Madison or Lexington are paths carved through a jungle of seething savage life, and that the corners of New York are stuffed with prostitutes, pimps, and murderous or illiterate juvenile delinquents, permanently dazed with hashish; but, in fact, when one actually does step off route, how mild, ordinary and respectable everything is. How mild and refined the dancing, how genteel the women's clothes.[1]

News of England from these papers is more difficult to get than I expected. Crime in England is reported, so are Princess Margaret and Churchill; not much else. All Americans, from all classes, say to me in the first five minutes of conversation: "Do you think she will really marry him?" They, or at any rate their newspapers, condone the intensity of their own curiosity by imputing the intensity to the English. "WE ARE WITH YOU, MEG, CROWD CHANTS AT WINDSOR. Through the streets a milling throng . . . etc." A pleasing picture. I can just see them all leaving the bar parlour of the Square and Compasses, linking arms and singing "Meg . . . Meg" to some old Buckinghamshire folk-tune. Another good headline, when divorced Eden becomes Prime Minister: "WILL THIS EASE WAY FOR MEG?"

In morning go with H. to Macy's. In women's clothes section she is impressed by the English export cotton fabrics, depressed because these designs for export are better than those channelled for home consumption. High standard of women's cheap cotton dresses, stockings, shoes, handbags. Good sales manners of shop attendants, well trained in sales techniques, big and small eye-catching displays, impression of choking plenty and roaring turnover.

[1] At the same time the existence of problem children here must be admitted. The boy Jelke did have this wayward whim—living on the immoral earnings of the girl he was engaged to, not because he needed the money (he was wealthy) but because that way his pleasure lay. Yet even here the basic gambit of U.S.manship must be borne in mind—which is to be just that one degree *more so*, whether in villainy or saintliness, death or love, games or bombs or aqueducts, than the previous world record.

Lunch at Sardi's with Francis Brown, Literary Editor of *New York Times*. He has given me a fine theme for an article: Review-manship. Nearest parallel to Sardi's is the Ivy before the war. The circumambience of celebrated stage people is rammed home by three hundred signed cartoons, rather heavy-fistedly drawn, round the walls. H. is becoming critical of food here; thinks the absolute cleanliness and hygiene have permeated to the roots of the kitchen with ill effect, the deep freeze killing the fag end of what is left. H.: "Food shouldn't be too clean . . . should have a lot of dirt in it, a lot of kitchen debris, a lot of sweat and tears, a few things that have gone wrong but which have been overcome on the spur of the moment; and it should take a long time."

Matinée of musical—*The Pajama Game*. This has been running for two years, so to New Yorkers it is two years out of date; but it possesses both the good qualities which make the *Oklahoma*-type musical. First: it has a real theme, about a real something (Employers versus a Union). Second: the music is really played, not tinkered at by a small bored orchestra, as sometimes in London. (Our nearest approach to good playing of this kind—the orchestra at the Palladium.) I am inclined to patronise the U.S. classical concerts and their habit of polishing chestnuts: expensive Philharmonic orchestras playing Unfinished Symphonies and Karelian Suites. I must remember that the goodness of American music is on a different plane, extending from the man playing Jingle Bells on the tinny upright down town to the rich orchestral force of the reprise of a Rogers and Hammerstein song in a resounding theatre off Forty-Second Street.

Dinner at the Auberge. "Delightful, tiny, inexpensive French restaurant" which Gollancz says we "must go to". Frogs' legs for one cost $4.50.

I continue to give her, and H. unwiltingly continues to want, full sightseeing days, crossing off see-worthy places as fervently as if this were our last week on earth. The 17th was H.'s morning in the Library and the day we got tangled up in the Shamrock

Day procession (see page 92). Then after Algonquin we thread through Shamrock to the Metropolitan Museum of Art, but only see modern china because key rooms are closed. Two guards, with live ammunition, tell us this is because on St. Patrick's Day "the children get wild in here"—the implied question being what, without the deterrent of sub-machine guns, could they not do? I then walk H. across Central Park, she numb in the wind, while I tell her how tender the green will be next week on those trees and how these slopes, now with all the life pounded out of them by the winter, will so soon be a pleasing contrast to the rocks—the bald rocks. She says that she doesn't mind what adjective I use, because her eyes are streaming with the cold. Then we walk down Sixth Avenue between alternating TV and second-hand camera-dealers to take the lift up to the Rainbow Room of Rockefeller; but the whole tower is so completely cluttered with American visitors, rubber-necking New York for the first time in their lives, that after peering over their shoulders in vain discomfort we go to the top for the famous view, and I point out the famous buildings waveringly because I am backing away from the edge as I advance towards it, owing to an inappropriate return of my old and I hoped disappearing vertigo. Then coffee downstairs and I fumble with change. I must rehearse instant recognition of dime, nickel, quarter, and get some real system going to separate, in cleanly organised pockets, the one-dollar bills from the fives and tens. What does the U.S. man-about-town do?

In evening link up with the Whiteheads. Whitehead is of course my old friend Ted; but he is also the man with the beard in the *New Yorker* Schweppes ads. Walking down the street with him is an experience. All eyes feed on the handsome bearded head of Ted. The fact that Ted, the Schweppes of the ads, is genuinely Managing Director of Schweppes in America weighs far less in his favour with U.S. men than the fact that he is really the beard in the photograph. Personal publicity is regarded here as an unchallengeable achievement by all ranks. The fact that it is

FAIRLY SAFE IN THE ARMS OF NEBULA

due to him by right of directorhood is an irrelevance, that he did not seek it an impossibility.

With Whiteheads to Stork Club. No comparable place in London. It is Publicity Castle, constantly on TV and home of Walter Winchell. Only three men in tux: two hundred not. Women in short dresses. Note: the English sartorial floater of unchanged man with woman in full evening dress is no floater in U.S. There are two bands, both far better than any we have in any dance-place in London. Beautiful for sound; infectious for dancing.

At 2 a.m. we move to El Morocco. This is the Café de Paris of New York, but without cabaret. Much darker, more night-clubby than Stork. More expensive. Girl in our party: "Gosh, I'm hungry." Kodex: "Let's get out of here."

Saturday, 19*th March*. A bad day. We flew or tried to fly by Nebula Airlines to Augusta, Georgia.

One would have thought, from the ease with which one can fly across this continent to Hollywood, that this mere six hundred miles would be like a morning trip to Brighton. On the contrary. It was the worst travel day, the only really bad day we've had. Reason One: the incredible casualness, carelessness, and unbusinesslikeness of American business institutions like Nebula Airlines. The airport at Washington, our first stop, is spacious, with luxurious leather arm-chairs, air-conditioned restaurant, enormous lockers for luggage, verandah bars in some of which cocktail parties can be and were being given, hundredweights of magazines on bookstalls, gift shops, patent boot-polishers, mechanical hand-driers, fans, personal telephone switchboard attention; but there are long despairing queues at the checking-in counters waiting on the whim of amiable but completely casual young men who shout down the desks confidence-undermining remarks like, "Hullo, Bob, do you know anything about a Flight 226 or something from Baltimore; isn't that one supposed to be late or something?" Reason Two is that complicated air-travel grazes my nerves. Reason Three is that my system of putting the right things into the right pockets breaks down under the strain of these conditions anyway. On this occasion also I was further handicapped (*a*) by air-deafness, so that the long sing-song of directions through the loud-speakers became incomprehensibly mush, and (*b*) by the misfortune that I had packed my glasses, so that while they were buried in some hold I could read only the flight-number and flight directions, on the innumerable cards I was pelted with, by placing them on the floor and kicking them a foot or two even farther away from my eyes, by which time the print had become almost too small to read anyhow.

H. spent some part of the day making up short stories about me in rôle of amateur cracksman or brain surgeon.

I have made myself forget the names of the places we passed through. We ended up at Columbia where "there was a connection to Augusta"; but we were told at midnight that there was no connection to Augusta; on the other hand they would put us on a bus, free. We got there at 2.30 a.m.

Sunday, 20th March. Augusta, Georgia. It is mild, early May here, and in fact the wistaria is already beginning to fall. But I note that these previews of spring, glorious as it is to see green, do not quite give the authentic spring feeling. Is it because one has to go through the preliminary changes of season first?—because the Englishman, at any rate, has to freeze before he thaws?

This hotel is a large, slightly seedy, country club; the grubby cavity of the swimming-pool is empty of water. Staff are tired already at the thought of work ahead—the Augusta National is in ten days' time, when Augusta will be full to bursting with big golf.

Careful introductions having been laid on, we set off to examine the celebrated course with jaws set as strongly as if we were preparing to inspect an exhibition of Yugoslavian tapestry. This visit is for my projected book on American Golf Gamesmanship. The manager of the course, to whom I could speak only by this introduction, looked and talked like a young university

48

don, and enjoyed no doubt treble the salary. The hallowed club-
house is low and white and pretty; two lesser chapels are dedicated to St. Ike and St. Bobby.

As a kind of initiation, we are shown the golf-clubs, fixed to
the wall with long explanatory labels, with which Bobby Jones
won his quadruple star—interesting to me, and unexpected to
find that most of them were made in Scotland.

I look at the course from the Golfmanship point of view.
We walk over every hole. The grass is like a Wilton carpet, the
fairway richer than Ashdown Forest's, the contrasting slopes,
like Sunningdale's, obviously preordained, when the world
was made, for golf, and there are wittily placed water hazards,
made by Jones himself and from time to time widened or
re-angled by him to increase the agony of the players and
the pleasure of the spectators. Jones was away, but the mere
thought that the first and eighteenth holes are in full view of
his front window must make those holes difficult to play.
Perhaps because Jones watches golf (and fishes the water hazards)
from his electric caddie-car, half the members own electric
caddie-cars themselves and drive themselves between strokes.
This was my first view of these highly gamesworthy objects.
Each hole is named after a flower, and most of them—Red Bud,
Dogwood, and Magnolia, for instance—were in full force. (I
shall call the middle holes of our Yeovil golf-course Ribwort,
Nettle, and Duckweed). It is a testing course, perhaps almost as
testing as Pine Valley, but unlike Pine Valley it is somehow
friendly to man, and the fairways and even the bunkers ask to
be played from. Pine Valley surely is only happy by itself, at
midnight, when wild animals roam and man is far distant.

In the evening we lay on our beds and stared for hours,
hypnotised, at the big TV set our room—each room—is
provided with. Watch Senator George in an admirably stage-
managed interview. The Americans are a nation of natural-born
dignified senators in political manner, but this one talked sense
instead of platitudes. A corny but watchable American horse

drama. Then stuffed in, as so often, apparently, to fill a late-night hour, a British film for TV export, well-acted but shapeless and incomprehensible, even to us—obviously cut somewhere in Manhattan by someone who had given up trying to follow the plot. Bad publicity for Britain. The commercials in three-minute interludes, so far from distracting, come as a welcome relief—three alkalis in a row, then four pain-killers, all "to give deep penetrating relief." Also, as we are in the midst of a Drink More Tea Campaign, for the next few weeks little animated figures will sing at us, "Take tea and see—take it hefty, hot and hearty." The rest of this commercial continues "and now we'll play 'Outside of Heaven'—a tune Princess Meg is especially fond of— perhaps she'll call it now 'Outside of Brussels.'"

Monday, 21st March. Today we take a plane to West Palm Beach. Our car companion to the airport is a tiny little shrivelled-up lady with a Southern accent like a plucked piano wire, who is taking the plane two hundred and fifty miles south as ordinarily as we take a Green Line bus to Reigate. She talks like this:

"Oh, what a sin you didn't go all over that hill . . . didn't see the hill when you were in Augusta. Now we are on Tobacco Road. What, you didn't realise you were on Tobacco Road, but there's no truth in that book. . . . I've lived here forty-six years, but I am still a Mississippian, and if Mississippi and Georgia went to war I should fight for Mississippi. Of course it's not all magnolias and tulips in Mississippi, but I wouldn't see my country down the road for anybody. We have all the records for the place, the Mississippi delta plantation . . . honest to truly my father, in the records it shows he came through from Duke Arthur. You wouldn't think it from my father, he was a chapel man and Duke Arthur was such a rare racy old bird. None of my grandfather's slaves left him, you know. They have all come down; the oldest one was called Marmaduke Hawkins. Of course my grandfather was in the North and South War. That was a funny time."

"It's difficult for us to understand it," I said.

"Well, I don't understand it either."

As we go south through Florida and step out at the little halts, it's warm enough. Quite fierce sun at six in the evening, the first we've personally felt for nearly thirteen months. The relief is unspeakable. No one here could realise how we feel about sun—really starving for it. Getting to Palm Beach at the end of a long day, we both felt a bit worn and jaded for the first time. H.'s normal—and delightful—reaction to such a sensation is to put on her most immaculate green silk dress, after an enormous bath, and we walk out under double-strength stars to a banyan tree, the size of a house, at the end of the road, and I am completely revived.

Tuesday, 22nd March. For my work—which of course is as almost always my pleasure—we watch golf: the Pro-Amateur Competition at Seminole. The fairway is made of crisp, even blue-grass; the natural features are palm trees and big, more or less unraked, Rye-like bunkers. How does it compare with a pro competition at home? Chief superiority is in the refreshments. We first tasted here the joy of iced cans of American beer. Burning sun at last—and, like a starving man, I overdo it. After a day of this my forehead swelled up like a melon, and I spent most of the week pulling off strips of skin like cellophane.

Snead was playing. I had a good view of that awe-inspiring release of force last year at Wentworth. The thrill for me was to see, for the first time, the dark, almost Indian-blooded-looking Hogan, playing badly but miraculously recovering with long clinching iron-shots, the ball hanging long in the air; Fergol, Middlecoff—all these golfers are browned to a colour almost sooty this winter. This year's winner was a new man—successful Souchak. A big footballer, Souchak walked lightly and crisply, planting his proud hoofs on the receiving earth like a P.T. sergeant, even after two rounds alongside Snead. For safety Souchak has learnt to cut down his drives to three hundred yards. Golf-clubs are like toys in his huge fingers, and beneath him the course dwindles to a children's playground on which this super-child is constantly trying not to hit things too hard.

In the afternoon H. and I window-shop in the "Mink Mile." This, built no doubt on an alligator swamp, is now Worth Avenue, the Rue de la Paix of Palm Beach. In fact it's all smaller (one-storeyed buildings) and less rich and expensive than a generation of Floridan publicity had trained one to expect.

There is a first-class bookshop, unexpectedly; but the astonishing and most delightfully satirisable thing is undoubtedly the nature of the "acceptable gifts." They make the luxury goods of Bond Street seem by contrast as plain and utilitarian as ironmongery in Streatham. There are, for instance, loo seats painted, loo seats quilted, loo seats with pictures of poodles on them. Dress-covers made of quilted nylon with gold zip-fasteners. Umbrellas with gold shafts and diamanté handles. There is a receptacle in the shape of a golden shoe with cut-glass ornamentation sold as "a cotton-wool-holder." A cat with a long neck to hold something else. Pale pink telephones with little roses all over them. No scrap of any pair of sun-glasses is left undecorated. GIVE THE GIFT OF A RICHER LIFETIME—A HOWARD ORGAN. The more tasteful ties, bathing trunks, etc., have, like the snootier cars, coats-of-arms on them. There are transparent belts, ornamented with postage stamps. The manly men's tweeds have pile as thick as grass; the rough jackets are like new-ploughed loam. In dumbfounding contrast the sports-shirts must be whimsical and feminine—pale pink silk shirts decorated with burgees and yacht flags, slub-linen coats, black shirts with a mauve design of cactuses or can-can girls. Underpants for men are of course nylon—most excellent—and the pattern has to be large insects: bees, grasshoppers, ants. For golf an ant design on ordinary white slacks is O.K. In the domestic fittings the general aim is to make the nasty nice, the unromantic romantic. Therefore the flit-guns, naturally, were gold-plated, with metal forget-me-nots down the handle. H. found when she was in another shop, a food shop, that everything was utterly and completely, of course, hygienically wrapped, but (as was explained to her) to take off the un-homey effect of the hygiene, bread was sprayed with a bakery smell; deep-frozen wrapped fish was sprayed with something called "Smell o' the Sea."

One evening during this time H. and I found ourselves alone in "The" bar—"Tabu." Here came an example of the perfectionism of American hospitality. A young man from Illinois and his wife saw we were alone, and, somehow realising we were a little short of dollars, made us dine with them, paying for everything. The point about American hospitality is that they have a real interest in foreigners, which they combine with dignified pride in their own nation. By contrast, certain English seem to bury their national pride, or be self-conscious about speaking of it; they certainly are less interested in foreigners.

Wednesday, 23rd March. Today we register at the Colony Hotel at 1.30—glorious peace, graceful architecture, air-conditioned heaven. It's 3 o'clock before we are eating crab meat at the pier restaurant. Four o'clock before we start bathing on the surprisingly unassuming little beach. Present on the end of a breakwater a nice change from a herring-gull—a pelican, a sort of old inhabitant in a seedy tail-coat, looking as if bred in some slummy cage of a travelling zoo. It flew away very slowly and gingerly, scarcely airborne, unskilled, colourless, like an old movie of the flight of the first monoplane.

Thursday, 24th March. I am coping with sunburn. The big bump between my eyes is blotchily red, but I have got ultra-violet at last, and here it is super-ultra. Unclothed on the sand for an hour, even my back, turned *away* from the sun, got brown. H. enjoys it, not without some nostalgic comparisons with her favourite Riviera beaches, where "a girl might find herself that evening dancing round a flagpole with a *matelot*; that would be unlikely here." In fact the atmosphere is much closer to Bournemouth than one would expect. There is in so many American women a deliberate and conscious disassociation from anything which could be remotely called abandoned or Bohemian. There is a general refining-up of female accents in these holiday places, a restraint in their clothes.

We spent much of today and this evening with two charming friends of H.'s. Unobtrusively they have a lot of money and live in a house surrounded by big walls and gardens and fountains, and the architect was the Mizner architect who was so effectively Italianate. H. spends time examining the kitchen. Of the endless sensible comfort devices, she liked best the oven out of which the roasting joint slides forward into view, *and reach*, as you open the door. The fifteen-year-old son has beautiful manners and easy conversation. He seems marvellously mature and fully grown in certain ways. He also knows Europe and England. He does not boast about this, but appraises in quiet little phrases. Sometimes he dispraises. Brighton? The piers are rotten. Your drugstores? They sell nothing but scent and soap. But he gave one reason for not liking England which I shall remember—"They don't like young people," he said. What a fine subject for discussion.

We were taken to see a training pre-season baseball game at the Connimac Field. This is a spring training H.Q. of Kansas City "A's". They were playing Baltimore Orioles—all very minor baseball. The stadium was tinny and flimsy. I learnt how to score, and I learnt why they had to be physically such big specimens—that you have to be strong to hit a baseball. I also understood that this struggle, to get a place in the team, was a crucial one—that $15,000 a year minimum is involved. You may retire worth a million. The hit with the baseball bat is deeply satisfactory to watch, a noisy, smashing, poised thwack. Suddenly Buster realised it was going to rain, and to our surprise almost ordered us to go back to the cars. We just got there before the rain gushed and poured and ripped; gutters spouted, cars stood in lakes, moving cars turned on sidelights. "First drop of rain for six weeks: may just be in time to save the grapefruit," they said. But it made me realise that Far South could suddenly bite—could be an enemy.

Friday, 25th March. Fly in morning over the Gulf of Mexico, towards New Orleans, H. enthralled by the beauty.

The wrinkled sea beneath us crawls. No, it looks as fixed as roughened glass. Has some writer of great descriptive power really described nature from 25,000 feet? Then there was the bringing to life of the map of the Mississippi delta. The gradual oncoming of land. To begin with, flat mud-patches which seemed to be floating first like water-lily leaves, then like pancakes; then islands, barely inhabited; then thin mainland, tacked into place by spidery roads. The journey from the airport to New Orleans is through miles of negro quarter. There is no doubt about coloured segregation below Virginia. In fact white segregation is just as obvious. In the South the negroes, forced together, have acquired more racial pride and in some sense more status. A large notice will say: "This is Sophisba—Welcome to the Finest Negro Colony in the World."

We are going to do New Orleans in the English way—i.e. at ten times the speed of an American doing its counterpart in Europe. Our hotel is standard, huge ordinary business-type—very depressing. We stand on the edge of the Mississippi and stare at the thick chocolate surface edging forward. In the French quarter we linger for hours. Antoine's, being the most famous restaurant in the U.S.A., has a queue thirty yards long and four deep—so we don't go there. Against nature to queue for caviare. Instead we have an average dinner in the garden of the "Court of the Two Sisters," a little draughty, where Palm Court, Astaire-Rogers music is being played refinedly. But outside in Bourbon Street, H., who was beginning to say "the playing is just the same here as everywhere else," is quelled. The point is that, even in the small bars, they are playing jazz rhythm which is purer and less westernised than any we hear in England. Or perhaps England somehow kills it. I don't think the repertoire has been much changed in thirty years, nor the performers. The best combination seems to be pianist and double-bass, with long solo passages for each. To pay for one's seat in the bar it is code to order a drink every half-hour.

Of course we go in to see a strip show. These large healthy

girls, some of them handsome, talk off-handedly to customers while stripping. Some amuse themselves by self-parody.

Saturday, 26th March. Preparing for a second day in New Orleans: but realise that all banks are shut, so can't get any more money. Also, caught by the bad luck which so often follows deliberate sun-seekers, we face the coldest March day in New Orleans for forty years. Cold air straight from the Yukon is blasting the fruit crop. H. longs for her fur coat, left in N.Y. City. Traffic cops are trembling in their thin cotton uniforms, so I, with brilliant ad-hocism, cancel tonight's hotel reservations and book 8.15 p.m. for Washington. In order to do this, I have to get either Phineas Farr or Hugh Troy in Washington on extremely incomplete data. In spite of the fact that only temporaries are working on the long-distance network, because of a telephone operators' strike, the Enquiries go gaily and humorously into battle and produce the two numbers in five minutes. "Did you time me?" the girl asks triumphantly. This is the best telephone service in the world. U.S. at its best here. We book rooms at the Hay Addams.

We spend rest of day in New Orleans window-shopping and lunching at Arnaud's, second only to Antoine's. I first drank sazarac (whisky, and the glass rubbed round with absinthe). What we ate was called Ham Steak Hawaiian, thick, tender, and brown, with sweet potatoes and the sauce *à la Germaine* —a specially wondrous yellow sauce made with white wine and champagne with a slice of pineapple on the top. The serving struck me as pretty quick and perfunctory, as if Arnaud's had a special manner with trippers and foreigners. No great care taken bringing us the treasured dish. I should say that the excellent food in these famous restaurants, best in the States, is nearly half as good as the best French restaurants, but the service is inferior; cost—a little less. No proper wine. Then we go and gaze and gaze at Snookums Mathews playing Dixieland with such constantly and organically growing *brio* that it makes even B., of London, W.1, sound by comparison like a boy running a stick along railings. H., for the journey, is reading *The King's Peace*. She says she is not going to read one single more American magazine. Cannot bear the feeling that she is being trained to take her part in any conversation on any interesting subject.

Note: the attitude to jazz here is rather like our late nineteenth-century attitude to Wordsworth. In other words, its importance is beyond the possibility of question.

Sunday, 27th March. Washington. H. didn't, in fact, read in the plane, but slept like a log all the way, as I did. Three a.m.: arrive at the perfect hotel comfort of Hay Addams. On our way down South the only good moment on that bad day was the hour we spent looking at the Mellon pictures here between planes. We had another very long go this afternoon in this peaceful, spacious, beautiful gallery of beauty, with cool, ferny courts.

Superb welcome from the Troys this evening. Hugh taller than ever, tenderly shining, like some eolithic dawn, softly mad, insinuatingly looming. Pat, his wife, makes one of those glorious speeches to me beginning, "If you only knew how much . . ." (She smiled at something I wrote.) This sort of thing warms me up for a week. The Troys are perfectly interested, perfectly appreciative, perfectly unselfish, perfectly helpful; and his marvellous stories have to be coaxed out of him.

Monday, 28th March. The members of the Super Spy department here always say they are "going to the Navy Office," slip away, and go furtively to the back entrance—of the Navy Office. A good ploy is to say, "I work for the" (split second pause) "Navy Department." H. has hair done and it costs her £4 12s. 6d.

Note in these hotels the comforts which are standard here and only occasional in England, e.g.: Cleanness. Lifts quick and plenty. Private bathrooms with shower. Iced water in vacuum. Store of soap and matches in room. Plenty of comfortable chairs. Glass-topped tables. Telephone service quick. Good travel bureau and shops in foyer. A thick growth of coat-hangers in the big cupboards. Doors all opening in the same way. Good quick washing, pressing, and valeting. Soup-platefuls of orange-juice and grapefruit-juice. *Washington Post* left outside door.

Tuesday, 29th March. Pleasantly interviewed by Warren Urra, of *Post*, on Gamesmanship. Thence to pick up Phil Graham, owner of *Washington Post*, and Brunck, owner of newly merged Statler and Mayflower Hotels, to be driven by them to Burning Tree, Eisenhower's course.

How efficient is America? On way Brunck tells me of two leaks in expenditure he stopped this week. (1) Thirteen months ago the order was given that all lifts should run at full power all night because Harry Truman was playing poker till the small hours somewhere aloft. They had run at full power all night ever since. (2) The man specially employed at £600 a year to make an analysis of the eats and drinks checks for Mr. Azek. Mr. Azek died six years ago and the analyses were forwarded by his former secretary to the catering department and filed. No one had ever looked at them, including, probably, Mr. Azek—not even when he was alive.

Burning Tree is another fine golf-course. Very like Woking in length and character, only more spacious. The gamesmanship gambits peculiar to this course were obvious; and their formulation gave me much pleasure. I shall base them on the Celebrated Member ploy. The guest must be made to feel that the President is, "we believe," playing a little way behind us. "One thing—don't *look* at him, please, and keep going—he moves quite fast and he's probably playing with the pro. And by the way, that guy with the golf-bag—it's really a machine-gun."

As we were putting on the eighteenth we were startled—by the sound of a machine-gun. Green woodpecker.

Brunck invited us to dine and dance at his Embassy Rooms, Statler Hotel. Food and comfort first class. We then go to early Chaplin. These earliest films of his, before he was in control, are seldom seen—perhaps because they can be very unfunny indeed. But I am glad that the cloud which hangs, here, over Chaplin's reputation has put no stop to Chaplin revivals.

Wednesday, 30th March. Lovely mild sun and H. takes my ancient hand in hers as we walk round the cherry blossom lake (the late frost has half spoilt it, but it's still terrific) and the sun lies softly on white stone and on the vistas and on the Lincoln memorial. Lincoln, in stone, sits with such unmelodramatic dignity, hands so relaxed, such far-away-looking eyes. And note that *this* kind of art—literary sculpture and likeness portraiture—is better here than in Europe, where the best sculptors think of it as a dead end, or waste of time, so that the job is left to second-rate slickers-up like R—— Z——. It is interesting to watch the purposeful tourists mixing with idle walkers on the steps of the memorial, aimlessly chattering girls in shorts, everybody photographing everybody else; and then inside by the statue they all become silent. I feel proud of this place.

The Washington Memorial is just *big*, though the Americans are good at being just big, too; and it certainly fits the vista of this sacred area—so sacred that we both suffered from complete absence of loos. We go to the museum to look at the Whistlers and his Peacock Room—all essential for the study of Whistler; but his oil portraits are worth a thousand Whistler decorations, or fifty nocturnes. At another party there is a division between the pro- and the anti-televiewing factions, partly because of the irritation latent in dry martinis, partly because our very good host divides the party into two camps by himself insisting on watching TV. As the subject is Oscar Awards, compèred very funnily by Bob Hope, and as I have never seen this modest-smiles and glittering self-effacement occasion before, I watch too.

Thursday, 31st March. Leave Washington, our last plane-flight before H. returns. Nebula Airlines as a parting gift said "arrive at eleven at Newark." Enquiry showed he meant twelve at La Guardia. H.'s unsuppressed scorn endangers my ability to get away with excess baggage.

At the Museum of Modern Art we see "The Family of Man" photographic exhibition. Some of the reproductions are the size of a wall, and it's all people, people, people. People in love, being cruel, being political, being lonely, being children; child-birth, illness. Some of them tragic and moving and solemn. Extraordinary tribute to international photographic genius (the Americans are still second to the French) and a tribute to America's excellent Public Institution habit of being about the people for the people.

H. changes into best black cocktail dress to drink at what I hoped would be a good bar—Waldorf Astoria—now out of season and profoundly unsmart, the men particularly looking misshapen in their sloppy light clothes—suits constructed to make them look bigger than they are. It's only men's sports clothes and labourers' clothes which are better than ours.

Eat at a Hamburg Heaven and then go to Birdland, where for double the price of the best Covent Garden seats we listen—for hours if we had liked—to hot jazz played by the best possible orchestras, sometimes ten trumpets fortissimo ten yards in front of our faces. Rather satisfying and soothing. A connoisseur audience listening silently and seriously.

Friday, 1st April. We very pleasantly lunch (twelve people) at the Weybrights'. Weybright is the Allen Lane of U.S. Only slight difference is that, typical U.S., he mixes in a lot of more "popular" material, including some strong sex novels with his classics. Over here nobody thinks that "a pity" or in any way wrong. His paperbacks are shinier and more strongly bound than Penguins. Gollancz talks of the relative efficiency of U.S. and English publishing. It looks as if the economics of waste worked here too—there are a wasteful number of five-to-ten-thousand-dollar a year executives just below the top. This is my experience too—certain big magazines, for instance, seem to be great believers in having apparently under-worked, possibly overpaid ideas-men all round the place. Gollancz and Weybright also compared with practised financial precision the incomes and cost of living in G.B. and U.S. The answer in these arguments, as usually, seems to be that the "real" incomes are the same but the Americans have better iceboxes.

We go to 57th Street—Hammacher Schlemmer, the Peter Jones of New York. Here again of course the "iceboxes are better," i.e. of course the celebrated kitchen comforts. H. particularly impressed by washable nylon fringes for bed-ends and the range of nylon sheets and pillow-cases with roses all over them. Great question is how would I look against a rose pattern? Unexpected was the goodness of much of the design; the knives and forks, the beautiful wood and Japanese curves of salad bowls. I bought a tray specially painted to match beautifully designed tumblers.

Saturday, 2nd April. H. starts day badly by turning on the shower instead of the bathtap and so soaking her head. Every English person in America does this twice a week.

This is a great day for continuing my pursuit of major American golf-courses. I played today on the most major of all —Pine Valley, most beautiful, most difficult. Cut out of virgin woodland, Pine Valley's fairways, never parallel, narrow between awe-inspiring rough, demand some of the most difficult par four, three, *and five* holes in the world. Severely limited membership and, I would have thought, difficult to gate-crash.

But my thought or wish was overheard last week by the sister of the wife of the son of a former amateur State champion. Result—I was telephoned. Please to take train to Philadelphia, taxi to Pine Valley.

The wonderful trains!—with their smokelessness, smoothness, draughtless air-conditioning, just too warm; their tidiness and the general effect of being drawn along inside a warm snake. Yet it is just this which makes me homesick, and wish I were being irritated by delays in a third class carriage on the Yeldham branch line, the window falling open because the strap doesn't work, and a blast of cheerful smoke shoving now and then into my face.

Taxi to Pine Valley; and now the great In Reverse of what would happen if a foreign stranger turned up, even with an introduction, at an exclusive championship course in England.

First the Secretary received us. Then he personally drove us three hundred yards to John Arthur Brown, the President of the club. Whereupon drinks on the verandah, and we were given lunch. Then I play a round with the President.

The first hole is the easiest four on the course (about 380 yards) and I drove straight; but my slightly deflected second was just in the wood. No undergrowth, so why worry? No worry, except that every time I get my ball on the green this quite ordinary-looking surface somehow took hold of my ball, tossed it in a blanket, and then bundled it over the other side. I finish with a nine.

The difficulties of this course are preserved like the sacred rites of a trial by ordeal. My host, age seventy and looking fifty, was scratch. Having announced amiably that a certain hole was considered "the most difficult four in the world," he himself nearly took a three. In other words, the difficulties are fair ones. But a mistake is never forgiven. At the next, a famous downhill short hole, my distance was exact, but I landed in a shallow bunker on the right. To overhit out would mean drowning in a vast lake. So I took my putter to putt out. I have done extremely well with that shot on our Yeovil course. A sudden stillness descended on the scene—host, caddies, and a greenkeeper. I failed completely to get out. Had I succeeded, John Arthur told me afterwards, and I know he was speaking the truth, the bunker would have been reconstructed.

At the next hole, which is nearly 600 yards curving uphill all the way, I sent my first drive into the lake. Land was 180 yards away. But if I allowed myself to start the hole again, as I did, I was only eighty yards short of the green in three and took a six with the sense of glowing achievement fitting to a birdie. As I strove up that vast re-entrant, I felt like a fly in the Grand Canyon.

In contrast H. and I went to an interesting party tonight in a North-of-the-Park house where the atmosphere was Chelsea and intellectual in intent. A lot of people stuffed round the house and standing in the passages, plenty of drink, and the unlistening talk of the slightly tight. We saw no other party like this; but it confirmed my suspicions that the one kind of function where the American genius for entertainment occasionally fails is the little intimate one of more or less intellectual friends, bumbled along with seeming artlessness in the A. P. Herbert manner. H. and I are putting on weight with all this food. Our faces are like full moons, she says.

We went to the Metropolitan Museum of Art next day. The lightness and airiness and graciousness of this building. I remember last time I was here there were two special exhibitions—one of the Art of Strip Cartoons, showing the work of Al Capp and the rest, with big originals of their drawings; the other of modern female costume, including the evening dresses of famous society women in the twenties. Enjoying again the helpfulness and *availability* of this gallery, I began trying to analyse once more the odd feeling, over here, that in some respects things are more "for the people" than they are in England. Is it the absence of "Keep off" notices in museums and parks? Is it the good-natured way New York City allows itself to be periodically flooded with things like Shamrock Day processions and a hundred brass bands? The spacious comfort of Grand Central Station, and the welcome and classlessness of the train? The way Washington, D.C., is laid out fit to bust for the sightseer, the lights of Broadway, the TV shows like "Breaking the Bank." The coats off in cinemas, the shops where there is no obligation to buy, the courteous service in shops, the absence of disagreeable waitresses in drugstores? The general encouragement to see and admire and be guided round the U.N.O. building? The crosses formed by window-lighting, huge, on the skyscrapers, on Easter Eve; the giving people what they want . . . magazines like *Life* and *Look* and their concentration on people? The Stock Exchange always on view, with a public gallery. Instead of ROAD UP NO ENTRY in New York, the notice reads SORRY, BUT WE MUST DIG TO BUILD YOUR CITY.

In the Art Museum I watched a young African negro standing in front of an enormous lethal spear which bristled with flesh-tearing spikes and hooks, an exhibition of African weapons from Central Africa. He was small and earnest, with spectacles, and took notes. There are a great many Peruginos among the paintings, and as H. says, even the lions have the expression of sickly saintliness. There is a St. Sebastian. We rather seem, during our tours together, to have seen more pictures of this unfortunate saint, for ever transfixed by a multitude of arrows, than any other. But this time there are only three arrows, quite small ones. "I don't see what he's got to complain about," said H.

Tuesday, 5th April. Spent a wasted morning thinking out what to say on the subject "If I had six months to live," an extempore conversation with Clifton Fadiman and Henry Morgan, for broadcasting.

These old, sound, N.B.C. studios, steam radio, seem older and tattier than Broadcasting House: an atmosphere of sadness and lost interest, as if radio didn't matter any more—old studio furniture with makeshift old screens and nobody paying much attention. I am not good at these impromptu discussions. My accent is only partly understood. I become slightly censorious. Fadiman is an experienced expert: Morgan is a TV star, as we realised when he took us via two taxis to see first the negro Harlem, then the U.N.O. building, at our request. Both taxi-drivers said, "Why, it's Mr. Morgan," and went into a long reminiscent chat. The negro Harlem is just like *Street Scene* (brownstone houses and they sit on steps in the sun). The simple outside of the U.N.O. building, given ever-varying detail and colour by the reflections in its vast mirror, is full inside of liquid beauties of curve, atmosphere, and perspective. Take H. to drink at "Twenty One." Now she has seen all the famous ones.

H. and I would like to have collected some of those Save-you-trouble Greeting Cards, a natural enough phenomenon in a nation where literacy can never be taken for granted. There are cards suitable for a four-year-old, a five-year-old, a stepson of three, a brother (very manly), a twenty-eighth wedding anniversary, a boss, a head clerk, a bedridden grandfather. At Lord and Taylor the good salesmanship. "Welcome to the Flower Show." "Bedrooms in Bloom." And little trolleys with small purchases attractively displayed and called "A La Carte News." H. says "cheap jewellery is no better than ours—ours has been getting better . . . nylon blouses here not yet really tailored, but those cotton dresses excellent and quite cheap, good enough for Henley. You can never buy anything as good as that in England which is washable. In London there's only one firm which re-glazes chintzes. Here it's easy."

Wednesday, 6th April. Today H. goes back. This is a gloomy day, therefore, and instead of getting to work as I must, I wander aimlessly among the Broadway sightseers. The practical certainty that I will not see anybody I know makes me feel as if I were entirely apart and seeing people and places through glass.

Thursday, 7th April. Lunch with Stephen Spender. As usual he has a clear, easy flow of original ideas, and puts a little muchneeded juice in my intellectual battery. He gives me a nice footnote for my article on "Reviewmanship" for Francis Brown: "Of any translation from the Chinese, it is possible to say that the poem is meaningless without the calligraphy."

I started the day very early with a memorable experience of American TV. I got up at 5.25 a.m. to be called for by a pretty girl full of the brisk and freshened-up tempo of cocktail time. I am to appear in "Today," the "Bright and Early" of U.S. TV which is actually broadcast 7 to 9 Eastern States and then repeated in compressed form 9 to 10 Midwestern. This meant I had to do my piece (an interview on gamesmanship by the compère, Dave Garroway) three times. Garroway is absolutely and completely famous here. When I got there the screen tests were on. As the first screen tests are made, the TV sets scattered through the building show nothing but images of nose-rubbings, back-scratching, yawns, and groans.

In the U.S. they are so single-minded in their belief that basic

TV postulates the necessity of the sudden impromptu pounce that I was prepared for no rehearsal: I was interested, however, and rather surprised, to find it was to be done in front of passers-by, who were already lining up to watch through a thick glass window at street level. I couldn't understand why they were crowding so expectantly until I realised that every twenty minutes the camera made a right-about turn and panned the crowd, who then waved and fluttered and held up notices saying, "This is Hiram of Ischiaville," or whatever it was. Maybe some father would be holding up a baby so that Grandmum in Capriville could see it for the first time. In fact I found the sight of these people waving across a thousand miles touching. It is a fine programme, and a few days later the Salk story broke on this screen for the first time, jumping the morning press.

In the evening Gollancz and I were guests of the P.E.N. Club.

Friday, 8th April. Al Wright of *Sports Illustrated* gave me lunch at "Twenty One." The general chatter was so high-pitched that I could hardly hear a word of the soft American speech of my host. His main interests, Joe told me ("you *must* meet him"), are dive-bombing and deep-sea fishing which, as I told Joe, gave us, of course, a lot in common; but he was very helpful and receptive about future *Sports* prospects in a way which I thought, as it turned out quite wrongly, was typical of the deceptive, the tremendous on-comingness of U.S. business-lunch hosts. Al was a delightful exception to the rule.

Saturday, 9th April. I am fortunate to be allowed to make temporary use of the Racquets Club. Easy-going U.S. talk-to-anybody stops dead at Temporary Members. Till Joe came nobody spoke to me. This was pleasant, and I got into the habit of coming in for a silent dinner, to read and play bottle-pool with the marker.

Catch the 4.25 to Wilton for one of those glorious, hospitable, and not always totally unemotional, week-ends with the Masseys. Usual fantastic welcome and glorious laughter from Ray about gambits. He is starting a Shakespeare theatre locally. After bridge D. and I probed each other's personal lives to the quick.

Sunday, 10*th April*. After the long round-up last night I got to bed at four, but had to read for another hour Lindbergh's *The Spirit of St. Louis*. I was astounded to find that from the book Lindbergh seems a simple, well-organised, and honest person—I had expected it to be emotionally adolescent, or stuffily "it was just a job of work." Far from it. It is a classic of its kind.

No golf because Ray's finger is in heavy bandage. He practically severed it carpentering. Much telephoning from reporters, much front-page publicity. His son Geoff sent a telegram which I liked: "Don't worry, only nine more to go."

Easter Monday, 11*th April*. New York City. Hot. Extraordinary to find almost every shop open. First breath of summer heat—and each shop suddenly has its own smell. Owing to the sugariness of U.S., the cake shop, instead of savouring appetisingly of baking, smells of stale sweetstuff. Drift into B.B.C. building and find practically no one on duty, except by chance K. and Y. They theorise crisply on why the Cunard service is so full of Americans going to Europe. Reason One: war-scare has moved East away from Europe. Reason Two: people are bored with the Caribbean and Bermuda, their substitute travel places. Reason Three: a lot of money—recession has departed. Reason Four: a forty-five per cent rise of stocks benefits not only business-men and stockbrokers but millions more, because over here even the watchmaker's assistant is an investor. Other economic points (I love this kind of fact or figure which, if spoken in a sufficiently firm tone of voice, can be made to look like the image of truth itself): if the U.S. was living now by the standard of 1880, five hours' work a week for everybody would suffice. Therefore to keep employment up two things are necessary: (*a*) The elevation of the art of salesmanship to a sacred and most honourable national institution. (*b*) A more or less conscious economics of waste. (One is not *told* to keep the electric-light burning in one's hotel room, but nobody ever turns it off.) There is an imaginative wastage of paper and packing materials and used-once-only cartons, etc. Cars are used till they are thoroughly run in and then thrown away. This is still an expanding colonial economy. Buy a piece of land and it must go up in value. In one economic sense each American man must be seven times richer than each Englishman because he has a seven times bigger back garden. All this is said so clearly and quietly that I take it for gospel. I enjoyed the getting-on-with-it professionalism and lack of loose ends about my old acquaintance Alistair Cooke. I watched him recording some talks. I like his dry, brisk finish. The Good Journalist. How the image of "Journalist" has altered in the last hundred years.

I like ASPIRIN written in large letters across the top of a monumentally dignified skyscraper.

Wednesday, 12*th April*. I was rather alarmed by my lack of ease today, speaking at the Dutch Treat Club. My hosts were charming and helpful, but I should have been much more slow, distinct, broad, etc. My first speech in the States. Only about fifty per cent of my stock speech-jokes took. Obviously tempo, emphasis, etc., must be worked out anew. One sound old human touch story failed completely.

This evening Phyllis Kirk took me (only she could get seats) to *Silk Stockings*—another fine American musical which will run for years and years, and then over here for years and years more. At Sardi's a table was reserved, and I was interested to find that P. K., through her status as an actress, had considerable power over this unattainable spot, particularly crowded this evening after an important first night. (Later I was interested to see, an hour after the show had closed, "our best dramatic critic" arriving simultaneously with an edition of the morning *New York World Telegram* carrying his notice.) After a time others joined our table. All well known in New York, e.g. Shirley Booth, George Axelrod, pale, young, handsome U.S. Rattigan, author of *The Seven Year Itch*, on the top of a most tremendous

68

wave and particularly able therefore to be quiet about it (talks about gamesmanship). Mr. Kronkite, most famous of baseball commentators, who at a word of interest from the stranger invited me to come to a game, with him as private instructor. Harold Ireland, sensitive and intelligent, young-seeming—it was somehow extraordinary to *see* the composer of tunes I must have danced to a hundred times in the last thirty years, like "Stormy Weather" and "Paper Moon," to realise that such feather-weight disembodied offshoots of the musical art do in fact have to be made, and laboured over, and are the result of sensitive, hard application.

I sat next to a figure who, though delicately made, seemed double lifesize because of her magazine-cover looks and clothes. Or perhaps I should say double clarity—because this kind of text-book beauty depends on the absolute precision of shape and placing of feature. R. F.—the beauty on last night's TV. Pale red hair, so immaculately right in her clothes that one marvelled she could sit down, and indeed there had to be considerable rearranging of chairs and tables so that her skirt could fall in the right folds. She made conversation with a kind of hypnotised correctness and clarity, like someone dazed by a deep personal shock. Every now and then she bent her head and whispered urgent words to her agent, who, like all agents of such, was dark and beetle-browed, with thick hair springing from just above his eyebrows. Speaking as one whose hair springs rather thinly, and from a point rather to the rear of the top of my head, I resented this man.

Wednesday, 13th April. I go right down-town to "the city," as we should say. The skyscrapers are visible only to the twentieth floor: above, cloud.

The many churches look like dolls' houses, at the feet of the skyscrapers. I call in on Douglas Findlay of the Stock Exchange. He is an enthusiastic guide: he shows me how the latest Wall Street prices are manipulated, adjusted, recorded, sent whizzing along wires and decentralised, how prices are flashed on screens, and how most of the rest of the work is done by faintly throbbing instruments—my first sight of automation.

After lunch he takes me to see the Stock Exchange. There is no question of being kindly allowed in by a back door here. On the contrary, there is a fine public gallery with two tall and pretty guides to show one round. Otherwise there is, as in London, the background sound of continuous loud mechanical talk, like automatic voices from a Grotto of Fun at a circus, and the fantastic litter. I would have spent a long time there, only words like "Stocks," "Shares," and "Securities" are clogged together irretrievably in a corner of the Unrealised Facts department of my brain, and nothing will ever bring them into circulation again.

I walked back due north to the Gladstone. I am fascinated by Third Avenue and the Elevated Railway. Although this last remaining "El" is only about seventy years old, by the geological time-scale of this city it is about four hundred, and there has been as much fuss, quite rightly, about the pulling down of these gawky, clangy pieces of iron as if it had been a treasured national Tudor heirloom. As I walk through the Bowery and the Chinese quarter, I am suddenly in a world of dirt, untidiness, weak physical specimens, men of forty looking like seventy, walking with white faces in a marijuana daze—anachronisms, all, one might fancy, as unreasoningly and lovingly preserved as the dear old "El."

Thursday, 14th April. Up at 5.30 a.m. to work on article and start the flurry of my departure. A dozen jobs. Excited to get five letters from H. today. She is back and they were written on the boat. The high spot was going to the Polo Grounds to see baseball with Mr. Kronkite. The first meeting of Giants and Dodgers. The Dodgers won, and altogether at least five homers were scored (and, footnote, it was also retrospectively about the most interesting game I've ever seen, because, as I followed baseball from afar in the summer, I was able to watch the Dodgers developing their first win in the World Series. "If ever I saw a team with the seeds of the winning spirit in them," I was to say of the Dodgers during boring moments at Henley to an uninterested listener). But I *was* interested. Kronkite helped me to understand something of the delicate balance of the game, of the fine adjustments of relative distances between bases, boundaries, and fieldsmen, which give this game its subtlety. It has this character, which I hold to be basic in the best games: it combines simplicity of purpose with an infinity of complex variations in execution. Again I felt, also, that the strength and physique of the man with the bat and the rhythm and wristiness of his swing result in the most satisfactory HIT, the loudest, profoundest, and most thrilling thwack of any game I have seen, not even excluding the serve of Tilden, or the winding up of giant catapults before the drive of Snead or Weetman. The ground was not completely full—it is always crammed for the shorter season of football here—but the attention could not be more concentrated. There is a kind of mystical self-forgetfulness about it, but the concentration is not gentle and relaxed, as at Lord's: the spectators actually shout. A delicate little boy kept half-rising to his feet and thinly yelling in a voice five sizes longer but no broader than his body words like "Skin him," "Knock his teeth out of him," quite unconscious perhaps that he was using his voice at all.

Friday, 15th April. Bennett Cerf asked me to lunch today. This happened in a typical U.S. way. Five days ago I casually told a woman journalist I had always wanted to meet him. Apparently she, without knowing him or telling me, rang him up and said so. I think he had just, and only just, heard of my name.

Cerf is all charm and likeableness. His office, built by a millionaire who went bust in the crash and was never therefore able to live in it, is perfect, almost too perfect, for a publisher's office. The house is modelled on a villa by Palladio. Bennett's room has plenty of light, flowers, panelling, books, etc. It also has cartoons of himself in his many parts—as a prince of radio, a connoisseur of humour, and a king of TV. There are photographs of his beautiful wife and of stage and other stars he has known in his work. It seemed very U.S. that the photograph of Marilyn

Monroe, whom he has TV'd with, was the nationally famous
nude of the cigarette (?) advertisement made in her early model-
ling days. This Marilyn picture hangs on millions of American
walls and is accepted as a piece of vaguely attractive furniture, as,
in other decades, would be in England a misty Greuze or an
antlerish Stag at Bay. Cerf has a neat, comfortable-looking,
simply cut, cosy, good-tempered face. He took me to Voisin's,
and I told him my life story on request, ending up with yesterday,
when I went to dine at George Kaufman's. He said that a
woman suddenly said to George Kaufman, whose wife is in
London acting Christopher Fry, "I don't like Fry." She had
just heard somebody mentioning the name. Kaufman: "I'll
send my wife a cable." Woman: "Oh, I'm so . . . but is that . . .
but if it's a translation of Anouilh . . . I like Anouilh." Kaufman: "I'll send her another cable." Pointless, says Cerf, to
quote these remarks without hearing the absolutely quiet, for-
what-is-there-to-forgive, dispassionate Kaufman intonation.
On Madison, Cerf pointed out to me the little man in shabby
dress with a pipe, who was THE publicity man here. He would
say, "I can get you tickets for that show," would pay $30 each
for them and say he'd got them for nothing. "But you can't get
really rich on such lifemanship gestures. Rothschild said he got
rich by always buying too late and selling too early."

Wednesday, 20th April. Sailing today for England. A very,
very bad last-minute rush, writing the *New York Times* article
on Reviewmanship and the *Sports Illustrated* on Golf-course
Gamesmanship until 5 a.m. Writing under pressure in the
small hours used to be good for me, and good for my work; once
I could break through the first sleep-barrier, I used to be able to
work well, but that was fifteen years ago. It was a great struggle,
last night, with my two Light Touch articles, even if it is lifemanship, which I like to write best of all. "Reviewmanship: or
How to be One Up on the Author Without Actually Tampering
with the Text." I quite like the sub-title. "If, as we hope, there
is to be a second edition, certain small errors and inconsistencies

can be put right." I am glad I remembered that good reviewman sentence. But I wish I had more time. Between 5.30 and 6.30, when it's getting light, I pack. One thing, I haven't got to worry about good-byes. Americans are marvellously vocal when you come: when you are leaving they have already got on to another life so to speak, and are enthusiastically greeting the next generation as it were. Joe, like me in this part of it anyhow, is against saying "Good-bye" as if there were more significance to the phrase than "Sixth Floor, please."

First to the *New York Times* to borrow a secretary to dictate my scrambled notes straight on to the typewriter. Francis Brown didn't seem wild about it ... not sure .. but I am beyond worries of this sort. Then to *Time-Life* for article Number Two, trying not to smoke continuously. I was long-loping most of this—really running from Times Square to Rockefeller. Traffic too thick for taxis. Must get presents. Must pay bill at Racquets Club. These last two bills, though small, just took me over my allowance, and I had to send messages to Henry Holt to get them to pay them for me and subtract them from my royalties. All this helped to make my exit rather a feeble one. It is simply beyond the comprehension of a New Yorker, however often they may have read somewhere about the hard-currency situation, that anybody should not be able to pay bills amounting to not more than £12. There is a drop in the temperature, if of only one degree: a hint of "H'm," as if a close relation of mine had gone bankrupt. But Holt's are used to me.

No lunch, of course, and by the time I left the hotel no doubt every other passenger on my liner was on board and unpacked. How far, far better I am with taxi-drivers now than when I came. This time I used what surely must be the universal solvent and basic ploy of U.S.manship—to talk baseball. My man talked also of his boyhood down-town on "Toity Toid and Toid."

But I was worried about the way I'd rushed those articles, particularly Reviewmanship, and kept going over them in my mind as I began to cool off on board.

73

But on board (this time it is not the S.S. *Tweedledum* but the S.S. *Tweedledee*) I must stop worrying about articles and start worrying about my radio and writings about this transatlantic journey. Observe. Note. Must wander off into the crowd and push round among the knots of good-bye-ers. The steward hits the gong for Visitors Off—could be quite a dramatic sound effect. A knell to some, an exciting reveille to others. A small U.S. group break into a little song done with a few shuffling foot movements in unison, and known, perhaps, only in some place like Egypt, Illinois. Something like this:

> *From Wilsonville to Great Land Falls,*
> *Onnesota Onnesota O*
> *We keep on seeing dose marble halls*
> *(scrapy scrapy scrapy scrapy smack).*

The last line is palm rubbing. The women are in their best bits of fur, sharpest heels, big, cheap, heart-disease-coloured orchids. Lots of laughter. "Remember Joe, Molly, and Joe. Remember Joe, Molly, and Joe." Single observers-of-mankind-type persons walking thoughtfully about. Stewards soft spoken, welcoming.

Being alone, I tried to get a good table for myself in the restaurant. I in fact asked to sit with the Gollanczes at the Doctor's table. The Doctor knows how to be host, though he has a rather mixed team to manage at these meal-times. The party included two men connected somewhat tangentially to the medical profession. Barlow was a sort of traveller in, or maker of, artificial legs and arms, very shy, ulcerish-looking, and depressed—completely unaccustomed to this kind of round-table conversation and inclined to diminish more and more behind his one link with social life—his Rutland Light Infantry tie. Dr. Abfelt was American, and had a roving research job for a drug firm. The only remarks I can remember Barlow making were these: "It's amazing how, if you can eat as much as you like, you don't want much to eat, in a way." Barlow, brightening up, because he was not interrupted, continued: "We had a little do in London for the R.L.I. just before I went away. A set price—and eat as much as you like." Abfelt thought that Barlow wanted freshening up, firming up, modernising, so he said: "You have the Sandover joint in your knees, Mr. Barlow?"

"We do."

"We have the Sandover Joint. But we have superseded that with the Chippenham Universal." Barlow didn't want this. He said: "There was another fellow at this lunch who had rheumatism when I knew him before." Dr. Abfelt sometimes saw himself as the Spirit of Hoover Missions. "Ah—you have cortisone, but as you know, we now have cortiosin which is sixty-eight per cent more powerful. We are going to feed you with it in rotation, Mr. Barlow, as soon as we have it in full supply. Mr. Gollancz, we shall rotate you." Barlow looked out of it, bent over his chicken à la king.

Thursday, 21st April. None of the public lounges here are as big as they are on *Tweedledum*, and so *Tweedledee* is, therefore, that one thousand cubic feet nearer looking like a ship. The waiters here in the smoking-room at 6.44 p.m. are primed to the brim with waiterness, and as we are not a full complement of passengers, their superfluous waitering comes out in little bouncing movements and needless busy-making jobs. For instance, no sooner do I put a cigarette stub in the ashtray, than this is poured from the ashtray into a super-ash-container by a special man, and these are in turn taken charge of by a sort of ash serf, who comes in with an ash-bin on wheels, which is sent in turn to an ash *peon* who, pulling a lever, ejects the crushed remains of my Piccadilly into the Atlantic Ocean. When I asked for the *Tweedledee News* at breakfast this morning, it was found (by a good deal of delegation), and then handed to me with a small intimate explosion as if it were a top-secret cablegram.

Try to observe . . . but in the morning I feel in a dream and a daze. New York City makes my brains feel as if they had just finished a tough game of squash rackets. Just feel capable of looking at the passenger list on the sun-deck. The names, I guess, are nine-tenths American, mostly first or second generation, one would say, from the explosive spelling of the names. Nobody I know except Gollanczes, Lady Astor and Kit and Justin Sturm, two Americans I met at the Masseys' and who turn out to be a delight. They are coming to England to see the place near Windsor where they first met or some damn nonsense.

I am very tired and half asleep. The deck stewards are too chatty, too amiable. An American almost as old as me but wearing a pattern on his sports shirt of the kind usually put aside for the curtains in the spare bedroom of a country cottage asks me, "Are you the Steve Potter of Exeter?" "No, Merton," I say. I should have known, though, that he meant Exeter in New Hampshire. In my nice deck nook is a man sitting there as if it is his as well—and blast his impertinence, he is writing hard as if he doesn't want to be disturbed. However, he turns out to be the nice husband of the distinguished and charming E. Box. I have written a note to Lady Astor saying that as there were six "Z.'s" in the passenger list, I changed to the "A.'s" for rest and refreshment and found fame and elegance.

What about my documentary programme and this vessel? Sound effects? No creaking of rigging, wash of spray, or roar of blast. There is a sound of somebody spitting out of a tooth-glass as I pass a porthole. Mrs. Sturm's accents are somewhat incomprehensible to our English sailors. When she asks for a Coca-Cola they bring her a milk and soda. I watch the delicately made volute of the prow wave permanently being moulded by the finger of the prow, permanently destroyed. I hear the small, intimate, open-air drifts of talk, aimless as Sunday. Ping-pong— people are playing it rather vaguely. Children, always faintly running. The deck steward with his heavy burden of politeness. Trying to move my chair before I am properly on it he makes little jokes as if he were a nurse and I was in an old person's home—"Old sun moves quickly, doesn't he? Oh yes, old sun is chasing you around, so you have to chase him around." My routine little squash game at twelve with pro. The special imitation runs and quick fussy steps of squash pros. In the distance some pet dog in the kennels is doing its pet yap. And all around and beyond is ancient, permanent, uninhabited wildness. It is as if a tea-cosy had been put on Uranus.

Later this morning I get a note from my old acquaintance and occasional golf opponent, Lady Astor. It seems to me it says, "Come to my cabin for morning coffee."

I must have misread it. Later she rings me up and asks me "if I know anything" (about mutual friends—political situation). I don't, of course. "No, of course you wouldn't. What about you? I hear you've been making a fool of yourself again" (my remarriage—she knows nothing, of course, about H., or about the circumstances). "My friends are all lunatics . . . and you say you have been playing on golf-courses and that's work? You are a lunatic. What news? No news? Ah, you're no good to anybody. I see no one. The Captain and I have a swim at seven every morning. Well, I suppose I must see if you've gone mad."

A good set of noises is to be got from the gym. The instruments there are based on the good old Edwardian principle of "giving your liver a good shaking"—shaken by riding a bicycle race on a fixed bicycle, shaken by a cavorting bicycle, by a horse trotting, cantering, galloping, A nice young gym instructor, bored for lack of customers, rather slightly built, rather delicate-looking, aged about twenty-two, demonstrates them all to me, then punches the punch-ball until his skin blushes with warm clear blood. These machines are for the fat women; and most of the wives of the American businessmen here are gloomily and irreversibly fat. Yet these rich husbands are kind and faithful to them, give them treats, and have hauled them out and up and away from a small town, and taken them on the glorious *Tweedle-dee*. I feel that the least they should do is to look after their figures. Too late now.

I have played through a lot of ping-pong games, to lose in the last game of the final to a pleasant French-Canadian who tried to and did diddle me over a matter of ends, thereby winning. This sweaty *Tweedledee* ping-pong.

Later I feel it my duty to go round the kitchens. The guide indulges a fixation on size and numbers, perhaps for the benefit of his all-American audience. "This machine makes two thousand rolls in twenty minutes. Here is the meat supply of an army corps. Enough canapés to last the Savoy for a week." Meanwhile all the American women make sounds like "Aw" or "Ow," up and down in sing-song unison.

In the evening I am asked by Justin and Kit to drink and dine in the little, smart restaurant forward. Certainly the standard of clothes there is different; and here, and here only, I saw one or two smart women. After a good dinner and good champagne, at half the Savoy prices, we go to an unbelievably corny film because "Jo" is in it. "Jo" is José Ferrer. The life of Irving Berlin with a sob in every five hundred feet.

Sunday, 24th April. I contacted Lady Astor at last today. She suggested meeting me after morning chapel. Her first words: "It's you who should have been in there, not me." Then for forty-five minutes we walked round the Promenade Deck at high speed, half-jumping over legs wrapped in rugs. She only stopped occasionally—to speak to strangers. To a mother, "You ought to play with that child more. It doesn't know what to do with itself." Or a seaman to ask if he was wearing the links she had given him ("because the Queen Mother forgot to give him any"). I had lunch and dinner with her. Some of her talk was at me and about my private life. She has the wonderful trick of being censorious without giving offence. I argue back, and tell her that although most of those who have criticised me have to my certain knowledge such black secrets in their past that my own ill deeds shine like pure gold by comparison, she is an exception. She talked about Plymouth and how it never got the raid kudos of Coventry because there was no proper Public Relations Bureau. "Churchill never said a word about the marvellous work done by women in the war. Why? He doesn't like them. No, he wasn't a help to me in the House. Why? He didn't like women there. He told me that if he made them feel bad he'd freeze them out. It was two years before he spoke to me. Of course, remember too I was temperance, but I do love the taste of rum." (I recommended the rum ice—she had one.) "He's been to Cliveden of course. I said, 'Why didn't you speak to me?' He said, 'When a woman came into the House I felt as if a woman had come into my bathroom and I had nothing to protect myself with except the sponge.' "

Of course, none of these things, nor her personal remarks against me, seem spiteful, and her delightful laugh seems to counteract and say the opposite of whatever she is saying. She says to me, "You ought to pray for grace. You are a nincompoop. I'm not going to talk about your affairs." I see she is interested and amused by the evolution and history of H.'s marriage bureau and its dramatic beginning. "Ah, but you aren't going to sell her to me." As she walks so neatly and briskly on her small feet in perfectly made shoes, she looks very pretty. We talk a lot of golf, of course.

We go to the Captain's cocktail party in his cabin. The floors and the pretty light panelling of his cabin are made, he tells us, from wood which formed the lower parts of the piers of Waterloo Bridge. "You couldn't have anything more English than that," I said, filling in pauses. The Captain, with genial paunch and short legs, sat on the arm of his chair like a hearty housemaster. "As a matter of fact they were made of American elm," he said. He was longing to get back for some leave in Liverpool. "You must be mad," said Lady Astor, and told how she said to a seaman in the war, badly burnt and not expected to live: "That's right, die and you'll never have to go back to Manchester." "It's a very nice place, Mam," said the seaman, stung. It roused him and he recovered.

Monday, 25th April. If there is one thing I dislike about these comfortable liners it is the atmosphere of The Company (in gold letters). One feels that the thing is run for the first-class passengers—and for the influential ones and friends of the directors at that. I had a keen whiff of this stuffiness when I was a cub B.B.C. producer and did my first feature programme: on Southampton Docks. But the crew, from captain to cabin-boy, have perfect manners and enthusiasm.

About midday we were in Cherbourg Harbour, a record peace-time run. Wonderful warm sun—and I am reminded that I am in Europe by the associations each place trails with it. Here in this harbour, for instance, I am back in Cherbourg twenty-nine years ago. A daydream, a lovely nostalgia, overwhelms me.

This morning I was taken round the engine-rooms very thoroughly and very deep down. I went in to see Mr. Kettering, the Chief, as we were coming in. So far from being excitedly concerned about the record good time, he was doing nothing whatever, or rather he was working over his list of New York City ball-game fixtures, Dodgers, Giants, Yankees. I am looking for radio descriptive material. Nothing in the engine-room for sound radio. The dynamo hum, the automatic bell as the water-tight doors are opened for my passage between compartments— that is all. Everything clean. Writhing, fat, white pipes like giant asparagus-stalks, and wriggling thin ones, in purposeful jumble. Coal would be so much more describable. The oil burners make less smell, I should say, than did my old paraffin lamp after I had made six shots at lighting it for my bicycle. The best sight—the propeller shaft, as long as a street, writhing within itself.

On deck begins one of those fatuous daylong waits which make nonsense of the "three minutes off the record." In the sun all the would-be sun-tanned are stretching their faces towards the sun. One woman sits still in the same position for two hours, unable to read because the patent reflector cup beneath her chin, for deflecting ultra-violet upward so that base of chin and nose shall be equally brown, is immovable. Surely a Potter-Grenfell dialogue here?

Lady Astor watched me giving dinner last night to the four Americans to whom I owed very much hospitality—now I find she has paid the bill. "I can't have you spending money on my compatriots." After all her cursing of me, I fix dinner with her and the Gollanczes tonight. Lady A. was good in her wonderful story about Shaw and his last day on earth; about Mrs. Pat possessively inclined to oust Charlotte; about Charlotte's adoration of T. E. Lawrence (Shaw explosively pooh-poohing). V. G. was good about H. G. Wells—H. G. wanting several thousand pounds for *Clissold* after he had had a flop, and how G. accepted but got his own back by bringing it out in three volumes. G. literally cried with laughter when he told how the agent, not daring to look at him, offered to sell the book-rights of an H. G. Wells film-scenario for the same fee. After Lady Astor had gone, G. tried to assess the exact value of her autobiography if she'd do it. He reckoned £20,000. I enjoyed listening to these two clear and good minds firing away.

Tuesday, 26th April. Woken at 5.45 a.m. Back in England. It is pouring with rain. At 7.10 a.m. we are waiting for a gangway. All these V.I.P.s and rich customers kept waiting one and a half hours because the Customs people must have their morning cup of tea. Can you beat it? Lady Astor left the main deck under a popping of press photographers' bulbs. "Go on, give us your best smile " they say. She was talking to three Salvation Army people, for a good publicity shot. Then she pointed her finger at me and said, "That's the one whose soul you ought to save." That was her farewell.

The rain, the Edwardian first-class carriage, the green grass and the primroses made me feel safe and sound. It was a grey day in London. The taxi took me past Buckingham Palace, where there was a changing of the guard. I squeezed my head out of the window to stare, seeing the sight as happily as any American.

PART TWO

Autumn 1955

AFTER the crossing-off stage comes, for me, the later visit and Stage Two. The relief of finding that it really is what it's supposed to be is followed by the first tentative realisation that it is something else as well.

Visit number three, in the autumn, arose almost by chance from that last lunch in the spring with Bennett Cerf of Random House. I told him I wanted to come back in the autumn because I had been asked to lecture at Washington by the Institute of Contemporary Arts.

"What, only one lecture?" he said.

"Yes—and rather an honorific one."

"But you mustn't do that—you must give at least ten. Where do you want to go? Who's your agent?"

Bennett Cerf was sitting in his office at the foot of the Madison skyscrapers, a building not more than two storeys high and therefore the most insanely expensive publisher's office in the world. Only Bennett and the Cardinal of the Cathedral opposite can leave their cars in the most exclusive parking courtyard in the States, although one man, an assistant in a second-hand camera shop, succeeded by brilliantly keeping a Bible, printed by Random House, on the front seat of his car while he left it.

"Where do you want to go?" said Bennett.

"Well, I rather want to go round the perimeter, with plenty of sun. The North West. . . . But I do want to see the Middle West as well . . . New Orleans again might be . . ."

"Will you get me Bob Keedick," Bennett asked; or rather he made a gramophone record of himself asking it, to be acted on while he was giving me lunch. He then told a different machine altogether that he would be back at three, and said quietly into the steel of a microphone shaped like a cigar that we should be lunching at Voisin's. And ten weeks later, when I was back in England and had half forgotten about it, Robert Keedick wrote to tell me the lectures were all fixed, the places and universities almost precisely the ones I wanted to visit. It had seemed too casual to be true.

7th October. I landed in Washington. It is about as hot as the hottest London July weather, but the taxi-driver tells me this is the first let-up for weeks. I begin already to dislike my luggage (its odd socks and the snap lock which wouldn't quite snip began to seem loathsome quite soon). I have far too many heavy thick suits. A good gambit in Washington is to say, "We have been sweltering at 80 in London" and take no notice of the fact that they are used, here, to a humid average of 95.

I was nervous about my first lecture in America. When nervous it is difficult to be aware of things interesting or beautiful outside. Whatever I look at seems threatening or full of bad-luck omens. From the taxi the clarity and whiteness of my favourite Jefferson memorial contrasts badly with my messy lecture notes. Robert Richman, secretary of the I.C.A., my sponsors for this first lecture, is looking after me, and he has to haul my stupidly heavy bags up to my bedroom; and here he is, I thought, stuck with another lecturer. I hang around his Georgetown house a bit and wonder where in London you could see such a full collection of Bach gramophone music. The modern pottery has tiny tops like the tiny heads Picasso puts on his torso-scribbles sometimes. Modern American paintings.

There were moments, later, when I could talk back about these interesting possessions, which were not designed to be passed over silently. But apart from being too taut to be interested, my experience is that if you shine in any way before giving a lecture all the shine is used up when you come to give it. I observed that Robert had stiff hair and a big head, a lot of strong face, and a big tweedy coat like my Fabian friends of long ago, and that he exhibits an attractive kind of calm warm-heartedness.

He brought me to lunch with a man from *Life*, and we talked about a gamesmanship-in-pictures article, and as I had already sold a similar idea to *Sports Illustrated*, all agreed with me that it would be good lifemanship to sell the same story to two rival magazines of the same organisation. But the thought of the lecture returned like the raven o'er the infected house.

The subject of my lecture was "English and American Humour Compared."

"If you want to think about your lecture, you can have this room to yourself," Richman said. Why should I want to think about my lecture? "What I should like to do would be to wander about Dumbarton Oaks," I said. I had seen this lovely park in the spring, with H.: now to enjoy it in the fall. But R.'s question put me off a little. Unlucky to start giving myself treats till the lecture was over. Besides, what about that middle section? Could I really leave it to the spur of the moment? I ought to take it calmly, jauntily; but to hell with poise. After all I had come pretty well straight here from Juan-les-Pins. My son Julian and I had taken it in turns driving the 740 miles to Dieppe in one piece; and then it wasn't long before I was on B.O.A.C. London to New York to Washington, including a jerk northward to Iceland for petrol, where all I could see of Iceland seemed to be given over to the Scots Guards Band, also aiming at America, for a globe tour of goodwill. This wrenching oneself about by air—I can never get used to it, and it scrapes the padding off the psychological sinews. Besides, although I've lectured so long that I take a pride in being able to discuss the Middle Period of the Sonnet of Discontent and think about deliberate fading of mashie shots at the same time, this was my first lecture in America, my first on the tricky subject of Humour, and I was starting with a crucial audience. "I expect you'll see a lot of peach-coloured bead necklaces," T. had said; but I guessed rightly they would be sophisticated as well as intellectual. Edith Sitwell and Aldous Huxley are to follow me next month. I determined to stick in my room. Anyhow, sunshine always looks to me like artificial light if I'm apprehensive. "Keep it gay, keep it light," Richman had said. "Speak slowly or they won't understand you. . . . I'm afraid we have to stop rather ruthlessly on time; a bell goes." My agent had asked for a tape recording; I decided against it. "No need to feel nervous." Normally I wouldn't. All the same, I felt like one drink—no good *drinking*, two hours before: or just before, either. No need to worry anyhow, because I had that first-class joke about the bad sales of my Coleridge book fixed for the first minute, followed quickly by the ancient Clemenceau story, which I fancy I can time right so that any audience will bring out that good fog-clearing laugh, which lessens the look of mistrust all round. If only I could see the third quarter of my piece clearly . . . I've got too much stuff. It was like struggling with an octopus. It's absolutely fatal to try to bolster up a lecture by having a lot of extra "good bits" in reserve.

"Do you feel nervous?" said Mrs. Richman.

"No—and I always think that's rather worrying."

What made me say that untrue and idiotic thing—untrue about myself at that moment? I was in fact frightened. Time getting near and I forgot that most American families drink nothing with their meals. "I'm sorry we've no wine" (earlier I'd been refusing a second Bourbon), "only claret. You can't drink a bottle of claret in half an hour." Only in five minutes, I replied internally. On the way to the lecture we left cosy sparkling domestic Georgetown for spacious planning and government department land, where every building seems to turn its back on you. I can't imagine that lofty Parthenon pediment smiling at my witty little bits. "How about a drink on *me* this time?" I said to Richman. "Doubt if we've time now," said Bob R. All the same, there was ten minutes for me to hang about in the hall while he arranged things. It was going to be a packed house, and a very hot hall indeed. Suddenly I saw a friend—a journalist I met last spring. "I'm covering your thing for the *Post*," he said. "Anything I can do? How are you?"

"Low," I said.

"Time for a drink?"

"Where?" I said.

"One block," he said. I was with him; but it wasn't. He was short in the leg and began to puff: one drink could have no possible effect at such a moment, but it would seem absurd now to go back. Here a dark doorway seemed to lead down to the furtive gloom of an American bar, but it was something totally different. On my friend led me. At last I rammed in a drink, champing it out of the glass like a stage alcoholic; but it was no good. It squirted out of me in sweat on the way back; and with my wet head glistening under the lights, it was time to sit on the platform and wait for the late ones to settle. Well, anyhow there were no depressing straight lines of unoccupied seats—no empty graves. In fact, some extra seats behind me on the platform were filling. Then I saw T., and I saw Joe.

There is a League of Washington Gamesmen, which is of course a delightful thing for me. But the happy fact of their interest in my work in this field is enriched by their manifestation, really out of compliment to me, of a necessity to try to be one up on me. On my first arrival in Washington five years ago there was that dinner they gave me, getting my name wrong and other ploys, and searching the State of Maryland till they got a butler who looked like an English butler in an American film and whose name was also Potter, and always getting his name right. Now I had written to each of these people separately and told them not to come to my lecture—that it was old stuff about the Meaning of Laughter and other smile-freezing, anti-humour gambits; but two of them did come. I knew what Joe would do, and did. He would sit looking in my direction just past my shoulder, fixing his eyes obviously on the extremely beautiful late-comer, the Indian girl who was sitting behind me. He did this; and of course a few other people followed his gaze, so that I was looked at, by a widening segment, but tangentially; and this tangent-looking is itself dislocating.

86

The start was good. The audience was kind, quick, and responsive. But the section I hadn't properly prepared, the one which depended on spur-of-the-moment selections from *Trivia* and Samuel Butler, began to labour, and I got hot again. Sweat stinging my eyes stopped me reading my quotations properly. I had to use my glasses for them, and sometimes I saw sparkles and occasionally steam. It was like trying to look through the glass door of a shower-bath. I held the paper farther and farther away from my face. Joe seemed to have shifted his glance to my ear. He told me afterwards there was soap in its hollow, from my last-minute shave. I relaxed myself consciously, and turned over two pages to my spot Churchill quotation, which I thought I knew by heart.

"Does the Honourable Member wish to suggest . . ." I am one of the three million people who have been praised for their imitation of Churchill's intonation; but as I was reading it now it seemed to me that my voice was as thin as a goat's.

I recovered at the end, thanks to some quotations from the *New Yorker*. But question time, which I usually enjoy, was rather a failure. I skirted an amusing gamesmanship catch-question from Richman. Then I saw T. getting up. T. was Hugh Troy. I had particularly told him not to come. This Washington gamesman is the American who has raised "practical joke" to a height so Olympian that a new name of greater dignity must be invented for it—a Trojan joke. He had sailed in, looking, with his great height, like a figurehead of Neptune on the prow of a ship. Now he arose with the mien and voice of Captain Ahab and said, "Would the lecturer please tell us why he is appearing in costume?" Laughter and applause. Of course I was dressed normally, in fact like Hugh Troy, and that was the point, and so it was difficult to answer. I half scrambled it, half did it clean: "It is surely considered proper, when visiting foreign countries, to follow the customs of the aborigines." (*Some applause.*) "Would the questioner mind standing up again?" Not bad, with the help of the good manners of the audience, and it all seemed to end happily—meeting the audience afterwards, then the hospitality of the Richmans and of the charming people who run the Obelisk Gallery, at whose house I subsided, with an enormous rocky Scotch, deep in the couch under a nobly lowering Rouault.

8th October. But I didn't quite get away with it last night. Bob R. pushed the *Washington Post* under my door and called out "Have you seen it?" in the same breath. "It?" Oh—a press notice. No doubt my young journalist acquaintance, following the press tradition, higher in the U.S. than in G.B., of courtesy to foreigners, would be too generous about me, especially in the lightly elegant local chat section of the *Post*, doing a *Manchester Guardian* to a distinguished visitor. But on page two I was startled by a headline: "POTTER (UGH! WHAT A BORE) STARTS ON ANOTHER LECTURE TOUR." Then words to the effect that there had been "the hunt for that 'pub' for a last-minute bracer. Potter, balding but lithe, tried G Street and H Street in vain." The balding but un-lithe reporter had kept his part of it out of the picture. Then he implied that I had been feebly trying to be superior about Washington, quoting my "aborigines" remark as if it was serious.

Pray God Bob Keedick doesn't see that report, I thought first. But what bad luck, that this perfectly respectable man from the impeccable *Post* should have chosen this moment to screw up the eyes in his mild and pleasant face, gnash his innocent teeth and attempt, very ably, a real old-fashioned Fleet Street at me. Work off my peevishness, chiefly tiredness, by walking round the Mellon Collection, the only gallery I know, outside Italy, where the setting and the hanging are worthy of the pictures.

Further rehabilitated by a small lunch today given at the Cosmos Club by Huntington Cairns, a practising Princeton philosopher who manages to be at the same time the effective executive of the Mellon Collection ("wonderful secret new pictures next year for our jubilee"). Under the Democrats he threw in an Assistant Secretaryship of the Treasury as well. He talked to me about some of the universities I was to see and people I should meet there. He was quiet, interested, and—like one or two other U.S. philosophers I have met—philosophical. These high university men seem often the pick of America. Their English counterparts are equally humane, but lose something by being less concerned with English life as a whole. Here the distinguished men can not only converse; they are even rather good at broadcasting.

I spend rest of day with various Washington gamesmen. Joe picked me up for a football game, but he had got the date wrong, so he took me to see the Pentagon, where he is currently working, but it is Saturday, when no visitors are allowed, so I could only stare at the enormous portals in Super-Doric, so plain as to be plain ugly, and a lesson in reverse on the subtlety and living vitality of more abstractly imaginative, less concrete, classical architecture. The quinquennial gamesmanship dinner splendidly organised by Joe.

9th October, Sunday. Richman drives me into the country for lunch at the Dean Achesons', where there were the delightful young Bundys and the Oliver Franks, he till recently our Ambassador here. Franks is particularly out of my line of skills. He has a formidable brain, able to turn from lofty diplomacy to high banking without visibly changing gear, and yet he is one of those completely tall, upright, courteous, serious-looking Englishmen, so dependably clear and so unwasteful of his energies that such a redundancy as, for instance, the use of gesture when he is speaking would be unthinkable to him. This is what the Americans like. The Englishman who can look like an Englishman and be capable and effective at the same time. The sun had an early September look.

The name "Maryland" is pronounced very nearly as if it was one syllable, and is pretty thus spoken. The fields of Maryland were like English fields. There was a cosy absence of wealth about the Acheson home. Lunch was a picnic in the garden, with the slimly graceful Mrs. Acheson handing things round.

She was inclined to want to know more about me, and wondered if we had mutual acquaintances in England, but of course her list of diplomatic hostesses was so strong that I could scarcely keep up at all and had to fall back on repeatedly bringing the conversation round to a few friends like Excellency "Edrikson," whom I did know but who was never very popular with the American corps and was notorious for the meanness of his Embassy parties.

Dean Acheson has a bristly, sandy, adjutant's moustache, and physically resembles, in his Englishness, C., our famous golfer —a shade less trim physically, but just that definite sounder something mentally. He is very sharp, very light, very quick in talk, without a touch of the public servant's permanent public address system. He believes the Democrats will get back, but seems to have no personal thirst for a return to office. Miscellaneously, he remembered how sometimes high-level political talk would be inclined to go on late at night deep into Bourbon time, so deep that the minutes would look queer next morning. How "Harry S." (Truman) was difficult to brief. If you said *"Don't* mention the Balkan Treaty," he would show no signs of doing so till just before the end of the conference and then come out with it slam—like when you say to a boy, "Don't stick peanuts up your nose at the party," and he never does until the last five minutes, and then there is some sort of tension and he does it.

Oliver Franks said, "But I always thought Truman seemed so spontaneous." "Do you see all that grey hair?" said Acheson, feeling his head. "That's Truman's spontaneity." They all seem to like Harry S., or like talking about him.

In the woods the *majority* of species of flowers are non-British, although the types are the same. This slight but consistent difference in look and sound (of birds) is a pervasive and subtle essence of foreignness. A small variation of clustered aster; a burdock with burrs shaped like lemons. (Both of these I found a lot later.) The young Bundys are gloriously gamesmanship-minded—they were never quite sure, when I suddenly began botanising, that it wasn't a gambit.[1] Natural History as an interest is not one-tenth as universal here as it is in England. I suppose because they are so much nearer the time when nature was the frontier and therefore the enemy. You don't Natural History nature when you are cutting it back or keeping it down.

A fine party at the Troys', and a final Washington incident. Hugh asks me to take Mrs. Troy on to supper to the restaurant where he could join us after losing the final guests. We start eating our roast beef, so much of it and so thick I can only prod it to start with, and we both also want to talk at the same time. Mrs. Troy coughs. Then she coughs loud, for one so smally and delicately made. A choke. I bang her on the back, and it makes it worse. She gets distressed. I have visions of God knows what. Tracheotomy? Too late? Hospital, surely. I run into street, fail to stop two cars. But a police car is coming—I rush across, just avoiding car. ("Thought they'd got you.") Explain. Cops leap to action. Before we know how it's happened, we are in the car going to the hospital, and the hospital is being warned and the case explained by car radio. And then, for all my anxiety, I am retrospectively thrilled by the fulfilment of a seemingly unfulfillable ambition. Through the heart of Washington at 75 m.p.h. in a police car with the sirens at full wail: like the movies. We weave from side to side, bodies in the back seat colliding with bodies. Pat still in pretty poor state. The doctor is ready in white. Asks me if she had turned blue. They probe while I ring Hugh. The thing is fished out as he gets there, and Pat is restored and immaculate once more. Naturally I think the American cop is efficient. So are the English; but superb as the English police are, it was pleasant for a change to do without all that dignity by numbers and that painstaking notebook. The cops took a few

[1] The Bundys are still weed-clearing in their new garden. Here I was staring vaguely at a familiar wild flower, and then realising, startled, that it grew at home on my own doorstep. This modest little scrap was a composite with a yellow pinhead disc and only four tiny white petals ("florets"), one at each corner. I was fairly excited because in England this plant is extremely rare and confined to London. It grows on bomb-sites, on waste patches. It has grown in a minute back garden of my own. It is called Galinsoga.

particulars, but they were easier and talked too; and when I was out of cigarettes they kept me supplied with theirs. That was their total reward—to calm me with cigarettes.

*   *   *   *   *

12*th October.* I am writing this in Central Park, feeling a million miles from London. The pen keeps smudging because of my sweat on the page—there is a late heat-wave; but 200 yards away 500 skaters are wheeling round on the artificial ice, and the sound of their voices drifting across the stubs of granite, the wild New York rock material, makes a sound like a bird island full of gulls and kittiwakes.

From Fifth Avenue other sounds—of brass bands merging and disentangling because it is a Procession Day. Columbus Day, this time; so the Sacred Heart Sea Scouts are out again and so are marching members of the Fire Brigade, the Dept. of Correction (i.e. cops), also the Dust Men, the Sewage Disposal Corps (informally dressed).

Last time when I was leaving N.Y. City I was with H. It was last spring and there was a freezing wind, and we got tangled up in another procession throughout a six-hour day whenever we tried to cross Fifth Avenue. That time it was the Irish and Shamrock Day; but it was the same symbol, the American umbilical cord incompletely severed from Europe: one-hundred-per-cent loyal Americans demonstrating to show loyalty to something non-American, and being all the more United States-like for so doing. Some of the marchers were pitch-black—the Irish blood must have flowed rather thin. The stuffing of these processions was made up of girls aged between thirteen and twenty-one dressed in satin blouses and shorts, their bare legs purple with cold. Some of them had banners which said CATHOLIC SEA SISTERS or WESTMEATH FOUNTAIN OF KINGSHIP. Thirty fifteen-year-olds, marching in strict time, displayed, as their backs came in view, the words HOLY GHOST, in white satinette on blue. This was pretty, and so were four very small girls not quite able to manage a long floppy scroll which said ENGLAND KEEP OUT OF IRELAND.

That was fun, watching it with H. But just at the moment I am alone, lonely, and about to be more lonely still, and much farther away. I purposely shan't ring up friends here till I get back, because I must work hard at my lecture, cutting out the dead or soggy bits and trying a slower, clearer delivery; and I must be keen and business-like about all my small jobs here.

But New York City *can* be brutally lonely. In a sense Broadway has the same kind of crowds and noisy fullness as the Old Compton Street and Tottenham Court Road, London, areas. But although more shops are open and the N.Y. lights are much brighter, the giganticness of it doesn't seem to be made by people or to belong to them.

The nature of the above "small jobs" is well known to many English authors over here. Though by some standards the rewards may not be so wonderful, to the lecturer who is determined to keep his tour comfortable and who wants to indulge in sorties and explorations outside his official route, these gleanings make all the difference between merely breaking even and coming back with a little in hand. Being on the spot, being a foreign writer actually in New York, creates a little ripple of keenness from editors and publishers and TV men, which would probably subside quickly if one lived there permanently, and is liable to die down fairly quickly after one goes back to London. I met A. S. P. yesterday, for instance, by chance, and he got quite passionate over the generosity of New York editors. Like me, he naturally loves it here. In fact he is a changed man. In London he is the quiet man in the club; but over here he sociably breezes round bars. I think the N.Y. women get him relaxed and sparky. After dinner he began to feel rather apprehensive. He's just going to do the whole of South America, three-day stands in each country, and do lectures, all Pan-Am. I remember A. once saying that air-travel was like walking in seven-league boots through glue. No sensation of speed. Of course the pay was going to be good. A. is very good. He didn't tell me what it was, but as we expanded, he began eloquently developing the theme that we were late Greeks, Byzantine Greeks, working for the Roman empire. I liked this, it made my suit feel less shabby. I'm sure Ted (rather modest and diffident) would love to be seen as a ruthless Roman exploiter. We certainly, as we talked, began to see ourselves as slaves of noble birth, our foreheads branded by banishment. Later A. wanted me to take him down to Ed Condon's, but the feeling that I had not yet done any good work this week put me against enjoying things like that. "I must go to bed," I said, and then stared stupidly for two hours at the newspapers in my bedroom.

Next day I got on with Business. This meant calling in to Henry Holt's. All the editors were out, but I said a long "Hallo" to Bill Buckley on the dictaphone. Set in motion my wish to appear in Alistair Cooke's TV programme, received a call from an immensely tall and brilliantly gameslife-conscious representative of *Life* (there is a new race of American young men who are just simply one foot taller than anybody else as a species, and proportioned as such; *not* unevenly developed hyper-pituitaries, but elegant and gentle). Fussed over my *Holiday* article on London Clubs, which is going to be difficult, because if there's on e thing I thought I knew about it is London Clubs, only to find, when I really get down to the subject, that my knowledge after thirty years is only five per cent, and that I really know nothing, for instance, of Boodle's (although it's guest-club to the Garrick). And for some reason Boodle's, perhaps because of its P. G. Wodehouseish name, sounds to U.S. ears as if it must be the essence of everything clubworthy.

All this is pleasant work. To leave myself out of it for the moment, the English author, already kindly disposed to his U.S. magazine editors because of their tendency to pay 200 to 1,200 per cent English rates, is further ameliorated by loans of secretaries, even of offices; by invitations to charming family week-ends. The U.S. book publisher will not pay higher royalties, but there will be hospitable and amusing lunches, secretarial advice and help, tickets for the Met., and even, during the first two years of its run, stalls seats at one day's notice for *Guys and Dolls*. The English author's nostalgia and gratitude for London and his London publisher friends is tempered by the memory of that one lunch every five years in a teashop, with cabinet pudding.

A good lunch was given me today by another huge man, six foot seven. This is Bob Keedick, who is shepherding me off on my tour, incredulously amazed that I have turned up at all (and always inwardly certain, throughout my tour, that I would never make the connection for my next date). He places my rail tickets for tonight carefully in the centre of my hand.

I told Keedick that the day I landed in U.S. I was gratified to find the streets alive with paper streamers; that it was only later I discovered that there was another excitement as well—the Dodgers, the day before, had at last won the World Series. So he took me for lunch to Al Schacht's. Al is an ex-celebrated baseball pitcher, catcher, baseball parodist and general extrovert of social charm who has capitalised on his baseball fame by owning a restaurant, being there on show, and displaying balustrades and furniture carved out of baseball bats and balls, frescoes of famous players, and match-boxes with the striking surface in the shape of a baseball diamond. He told us long, good, funny stories in a hurried, husky voice without looking at us, and then said his passion was for car-driving. "I like to drive to Jacksonville in one," he said. "That's a thousand miles." I hadn't spoken for a long time, so I said, "It's certainly a good way of seeing scenery." "How's that again?" "Scenery," I said. "I don't know about the *scenery*," he said, and went. But he brought me a signed copy of his autobiography, a good number for my "signed" shelf.

The chapels of peace in America are the main-line trains, and it was blessedly comfortable to get into my little single compartment in Grand Central, New York Central line, bound for a place called, not as it would be in England, something like Dunham, out of Domesday Book, and meaning dully "the dune near the enclosure," but Elyria, which never could possibly have meant Illyria or anything else. Name drawn out of a hat.

13*th October*. Last night I slept deliciously in my "roomette" —small separate sleeper with big arm-chair, on top of which a comfortable bed comes down. A child can do it (Groucho: "Ring the bell for a child"); but still, I did it. Quietness and cleanness of these trains; the air-condition envelope shuts out sound as well. Only drawback—heat is at least five degrees too warm for an Englishman, so that I long again for that real old English sooty draught through a window covered with steam and dirt and stuck half-open. Also, it takes a long time to get dinner . . . we sit in comfy lounge bar waiting our turn. Hungry, I was trapped into making a superior remark—one of three on this visit. It only comes back at you and makes you feel a fool. One lady had given up ideas of eating and was just sticking to rye on the rocks. She lived near Poughkeepsie (called "P-keepsy"). "Near Hyde Park," she said. "I live near Hyde Park, too," I said. Then firming up my voice at her as if she was a child of six. "Hyde Park, London," I said. "Oh yes," she said, "there are so many Hyde Parks." When I got my seat the food was very clean and efficient, but it didn't come for forty minutes. My ancient and tottery negro waiter kept saying, "I've got more'n I kin do," and seemed always on the verge of giving up.

14*th October*. Day of my first lecture: Oberlin College. Slept like a log, of course. After glaring, 6.30 a.m., at the absolute monotony and flatness of 10,000-acre rectangular, hedgeless, farms of Ohio, I arrive at Elyria. Carry my two too-heavy bags behind a coffin, draped with Stars and Stripes, and four weeping relatives to station yard, where there is a car to take me to the Oberlin Inn, room number 13.

This was a kind of *Alice Through the Looking Glass* day for me. The first day of Old England in a university of the U.S., finding everything recognisable yet everything different.

In order even to begin to comprehend this difference, it is

necessary to keep saying to oneself "Time Scale. Remember the American Time Scale." Oberlin College was founded in the eighteen-forties, so that by English university time measurement it is modern: by American time it is historic.

Let me underline this by repeating my first small but useful experience of the measuring-rod of U.S. antiquity. I was new to America—and I had asked my taxi-driver to show me the landmarks of Beverly Hills, Cal. Though a professional guide, he was in genuine awe of the things he showed me.

"Do you see that hotel?" he said.

It didn't look particularly much.

"If the walls of that hotel had tongues, it could tell you a story. It must be nearly thirty years old."

At that time the date of my home in England was 1550: of two of my previous homes 1608 and 1711. My own college quadrangle—Merton's Mob Quad—had been built *circa* 1292. Oberlin College was regarded as old, and in rather the same kind of way—and it had been founded in the eighteen-forties. And my point is that it *is* old, and its key dates (it was the first co-educational college) are genuinely far in the past, not because of the number of years which have elapsed since then, but because of the density of American history in that time, the number of events per square year.

First thing is to get bearings. *What, to start with, is a campus?* I was booked to speak, that evening, "on the campus." Did that mean in the open air in the middle of a playground? In fact, a campus is a large rambling square of buildings built round a central park-and-tree place, all very public. On the east and north sides were recognisable college buildings—"modern" we would call them, although in fact they are 1880 Presbyterian in style, and include one conservatory of music and one large looming chapel (where I am to lecture). On the west side are shops, grocers, drugstores, small but blazing with neon in the evening. On the south side is displayed the U.S. peculiarity of homogeneity in utter difference. Building Number One is the 120-year-old inn, made when this place was a safety station on the frontier across the Alleghanies. All this is being pulled down, the last remains of its foundations treasured and sketched by antiquarian students and relic-collectors. Next is the new inn, a completely air-conditioned and utterly comfortable motel, which is run in some mysterious way by the college. Next door to this is a boldly dramatic modern theatre, surging out of the ground in white stone, with a fluted façade in the jaws of its frontage to catch the low cross sun and therefore nicknamed by the students "Moby Dick." After Moby Dick it is fifteenth-century Florence. The art school is a delicate reconstruction of Brunelleschi's "Spedaglia degli Innocenti," and so a hundred yards from a gents' shirt store you will be in Renaissance Italy. It wouldn't fit in England, but for some reason it does here. Co-ed students gave me lunch at their co-op hostel; we were mutually diffident, and when they cross-questioned me about how to be one-up on their teachers, I was shy of them. In the evening the President came to escort me from my hotel (unlikely that the no more distinguished Vice-Chancellor of, say, Redbrick, would do this), and I had charming dinner with his wife and two beautiful daughters. One was a TWA air hostess who was therefore, perhaps unfairly, thousands of travel-miles up on me and could top Damascus with Hong Kong or Constantinople. Then came a warming dinner with a really good Mâcon, to smooth away my lecture fears, but in fact the chapel was packed beyond seating-capacity, 2,000, the audience very quick, and so I enjoyed it. A certain non-seriousness in my theme fitted, I think, the fact that this was one of a dozen festival week-ends. This one was called "Homecoming," implying to students who have been here a quarter of a term that it is beginning to be home for them. During my lecture I saw a vast dark figure standing in the chapel aisle. The fact that it was Duke Ellington barely made me raise an eyebrow. It did surprise me that his band was going to give a performance after my exit. I exchanged long and hearty handshakes with this genius. The chapel cleared after me and filled again for him—

less full because I was free and he was a dollar. In his tux he strode elegantly to the platform, diamond cuff-links and all, and I waited with the President to listen.

Lecturers must stem the tendency to talk harder than ever as soon as they've got off the platform. If you've been any good, it will make other people want to talk. The President took me back to the inn. He is unusually distinguished academically; so it is a surprise that he should look strong and handsome, like Dick Tracy if Dick Tracy were properly drawn. He said the light touch on the platform was a wonderful thing so long as the students didn't suspect you of being condescending. I am confirmed in feeling Dr. Stevenson must be good because he spoke of his mistakes. Once he had tried to be extra light, but a note of sarcasm had crept in and the university magazine had denounced him in two successive numbers. He then told me interesting things about Oberlin: that beautiful Moby Dick, the theatre (designed by Harrison of the UNO building), was, as I had noticed, dedicated to Sophonisba Hall, "mother of the Hall of Oberlin College," who had in his post-graduate work, in "little laboratories rigged up," etc., "discovered the process by which aluminum was made." I spoilt all this by saying vaguely, "Is that some sort of new element?"—forgetting that our word for it is aluminium and not accented on the second syllable.

14th October. I was so preened up by yesterday and enjoyed the Oberliners so much that I stayed on another day. An Oxford English graduate said he would play golf. In his first term, he was teaching the organ here; he was somewhat overworked, but spellbound by the U.S.

The nine-hole course played like eighteen—full of vast holes. Perhaps because every probability was against it (unfamiliarity, lack of practice) I got the number 4 on my card quite often. I still had the pleasing sound of the quick-witted response of those students in my ears, so I was surprised when my friend said, "Of course to us they seem extraordinarily backward when they start here. Take my music students, for instance. At Oxford a sound training in one or two instruments is presupposed when you stay there—plus of course basic harmony, general knowledge of Beethoven and the nineteenth century. Here one or two of them know a few of Mendelssohn's Songs Without Words, and nothing else. Of course they're very bright . . ."

"And they catch up in the end?"

"More so—or less so."

"But what about High School?"

"Well, they don't do any *work* there. Not *work*. Their day is over at three, then they go to the cinema or watch TV."

This was all news to me, but it planted a thought which grew and grew during my tour.

At 6 p.m. I was called for by the best-dressed U.S. student I ever saw—or perhaps the virgin pork-pie hat he wore was a gesture to show an Englishman what could be done. His perfect beard seemed carved in bas-relief. He agreed that High School didn't give you enough. But so far as the music students were concerned, I thought later, what English student could play the guitar so beautifully as the man on the campus at the students' barbecue, with students sitting at his feet and singing? This was prelude to tomorrow's "Homecoming" football match against a rival college, so there was a procession headed by (*a*) a band, (*b*) cheer-leaders, (*c*) the football team. Torch-bearers ceremoniously lit the bonfire. The cheer-leaders, young men and women in sweaters, went through tribal-dance motions which gave me arthritis in the knee-joints just to look at them. The rest stood round the bonfire in a large circle, with calm and absent faces, recording it all, already sad with the anticipation of the nostalgia this would one day bring them. I then went off with the organ teacher to listen to him playing two or three of the dozen organs of the music school. He belongs to the Walton loyalty rather than the Ben Britten. He plays Byrd and Bach well; and I stood over him, or rather over his legs, in his finale, because I had always wanted to observe the leg-work in the fugue of Bach's "Great" G minor, which I had thought of as impossible to the

human foot; but observation of those flying leather soles—
Orpheus with his boot—made me realise how runningly Bach
had written this for footwork. Why was Oxford teaching the
organ? Because he loved the organ, and he loved teaching.

15*th October*. This wasn't quite so good. It was only a half-day
stand, so I particularly wanted to give it plenty of time. My
alarum went wrong, and the man who was going to drive me
seventy miles to Canton for ten dollars woke me *with the car*.
A fearful scrabbled pack, and I was late for the Canton Women's
Club lunch. Canton is somewhat featureless, at one worried
glance. In some part it is "all a steel town." My Canton Women's
Club had a dozen charmingly dressed and smart women already
half-way through lunch. They were informal and amusing and
out for a good day. They "couldn't be members unless they were
graduates" of something. All the more pity, since I strongly
believe in the kind of post-marriage, later continuance of education that these clubs stand for, that I failed really to make contact
or be understood here. Without a strong leavening of students
I can't yet get the audience really going, and the fact that they
didn't laugh those good long belly-laughs made me tense up and
made them go flabby. However, afterwards all had tea, as a compliment to England; and we drove round the park to see McKin-
ley's tomb. M. was a good President, I believe, and because he
was (*a*) murdered and (*b*) a Canton boy, they gave him a
mausoleum three times the size of the Invalides.

Bus north to Cleveland, three hours. A frontiersman rough-
rider, in ten-gallon hat, went to sleep all the way with head
buried in my stomach (little girl aged three). Cleveland is one of
the rather withering business towns of the Chicago group, with
a meltingly beautiful symphony orchestra and superb pictures,
which of course I never got to. Vast draughty streets and those
completely mechanical hotels, anonymous—you are a man with a
room number, like a convict. A sort of well-trained machine of
"good service" is very freezing—no words spoken except those
printed in the Hotel Employees' Instruction Booklet. Along the

too-wide streets are alternate food shops and drink shops—little dark bars. Then "book" shops piled with second-hand girlie-girlie mags. A non-stop burlesque (strip-tease) show was uninhibited beyond anything I've seen in Barcelona or Toulouse, and makes the Vieux Carrée, New Orleans, look like a Jane Austen tea-party. This is called a Bump and Grind act. After almost stripping, the girls lie on a couch and simulate the motions of coition. One girl—a pretty mature one—released a final catch on the two discs of her brassière to reveal a pair of budgerigars.

It is now *October 16th, Sunday*, and I am in a North Star M2 aircraft heading due west from Toronto. I tried to fix such a route through Keedick, partly to travel over Canada (which I have never seen) and partly to fly over the Great Lakes, starting this morning from Cleveland, Ohio, over Lake Erie to Ontario. Suburbs of Cleveland no doubt look nothing on the ground, but even Suburbia appears fragile and delicate from 3,000 feet. As all the cars in U.S. now are pink, white, green and blue, the checkerboard looked as if it was scattered with tiny candies ("hundreds and thousands" in English); and now it is already late autumn here: in the copses every tree is a different clear colour, so they look like tiny tufts of wool on H.'s *gros-point* stitching. But to hell with description. My taxi-driver yesterday said, passing gorgeous tints, "Bad time to see the country—all burnt up"; a woman in the bus said, "Do you have autumn colours in England?"

We crossed Lake Erie, colour of lead, and my first air glimpse of Canada shows it already emptier than the States, more devoid of roads, people, and originality in names. Leaving Cleveland we passed, still in Ohio, over EUCLID, NOVELTY, AURORA. But now, in Canada, the names are KITCHENER, WATERLOO, SHAKESPEARE, and we land at LONDON on the winding THAMES. A quick Customs here. Then we are completely bedded down in clouds —and Toronto was just a quick rush from one plane to the other. Rather afraid my luggage isn't on. Vast Distancemanship for the global   aveller: Toronto is slightly nearer to England than it is to Vancouver and my next booked hotel. West for Winnipeg, cloud below.

Slaty glimpses of Lake Superior, and now, crossing from Ontario into Manitoba, the country is irregularly laced with lakes, gouged out by the Ice Age glacier.

17th October. Another lifelong ambition achieved today—riding on the Canadian Pacific. Winnipeg, where I started this morning, was still depressing. A shower of snow. "Never," I shall say, "talk about the depression of Sunday till you have seen an October Sunday evening in Winnipeg." Streets too wide—spacious about nothing. Here and there little warped boarded shops, sagging, dirty, belonging to the early settlement, next door to forbidding concrete banks and twenty-storey hotels; some trees, but winter has already killed the leaves, and fearful winds will soon be blowing down streets rigid as rail tracks, thrusting against the windows of the big, bleak shops. The hard shop-window lights glare on a lot of rather expensive rubbish, as if trinkets for Indians.

How uncosy are these towns. The people rather bleak and sad, as if they vaguely felt they were missing something by being on the edge of things. For the first time in my life I saw a man dressed as a cowboy—who was a cowboy, not a film actor or a boy of six. Working men wear those good tough check shirts and look really tough, not actor-tough, like some types of U.S. masculinity.

Catch 10 o'clock a.m. for Vancouver. This will take forty-six hours. I have got (no "roomettes" vacant) a "bedroom." Private loo, and bed and chairs enough for two. Great luxury. Today will be pretty dead straight across the prairie (the line disappears behind in infinite straight perspective, till it dips over the curve of the earth). Tomorrow we are on the twistiest rail-track in the world, over the high ridge of the Rockies.

Good thing about the C.P.R. is, so far, perfect cleanness . . . no crowd—the 400-yard train seems to be only a quarter full . . . the lord-of-the-earth feel of sitting in the front of an "observation dome," in which, above the train and surrounded by glass, I am reminded of my astro-hatch thrill when I once, on peacetime business, flew low round all the islands of the Scottish coast in an old Sunderland bomber. The food is fine (tea and English cigarettes in Canada, thank God).

Surprise of C.P.R. There is no splendid baroque engine with clanging bells and largesse of steam and noise—these are for freight trains only and luckily there are plenty of these. We have a pair of faintly fuming diesel engines only. Strange also that we amble along at never much more than forty and stop at most "stations" (stations are simply railside granaries and a few wooden houses). In some respects it must be pleasantly the same as seventy years ago.

Outside the window I see "prairie," I suppose, first cultivated then wild; fenceless squares through Ontario, rolling and swampy this afternoon in Saskatchewan. It is cursed and end-of-the-earth-like, partly because in my eyes signs of early winter *now* seems landscape madness. No green anywhere except in winter shoots: everything struck dead twice over—first by drought, second by winter. Plants the colour of skeletons in bright sun; bare earth sooty black from the deliberate burning of stubble and from chance burnings continually flaming along the track—flames prodded into control long-sufferingly by labour gangs. But also the ploughed surface is black, too, and this dirt soil must be *loess* itself: glacier dust ground by the weight of the old mile-thick glacier. Mr. Polly would call this whole route very geology.

A fine first-class road alongside the railway. No houses except near stations, where they are like dolls'-houses—particularly as their pre-fab walls are stamped with patterns of imitation brick or tiles. A little compressed bijou porch, a front-door with door-knob and bell, and a spaniel sitting in the middle of the doorstep look strange stuck up very straight in the middle of the prairie.

18th October. This was supposed to be *the* day, and was, crossing the Rockies. Only danger, mists, but weather right . . .

the burst-open mountain landscape, with furious outlines, was softened by October sun, sun catching tops of mountains, cross-graining snow-slopes, shining through dead poplar and, soon, through living birch-leaves (because on the Pacific side the season turned back from early winter to autumn); sun cobwebbing the telegraph wires; and the basic of all nature contrasts, hard mountain and soft cloud. Trails of cloud round the foot of the peaks wreathe these old barnacles in chiffon.

Today started at seven by my waking at Calgary; still prairie, flat. I get into the observation car right away, and watch each step Rockywards. Bumps become mounds become dunes become hillocks become high ridges, downs, hills, so into clashing, crashing peaks in jagged desolate brown ridges, caster-sugared with snow. Geologically and ecologically these mountains are splendidly simple: the "tip" (towards the Pacific) is so obvious, and the ecological rush-line, lichen-line, fir-line thins away evenly like a good hair-cut.

We are all excited by this grandeur, but have no grandeur of self-expression to match it. I don't think the word "cute" was actually used, but "intriguing" was; and a woman who had been silent all yesterday was stimulated by the scene into delivering herself of an indignant monologue about getting her passport for the U.S.A. "Not only did they take my fingerprints" (she was so breathlessly respectable and had such a lot of expensive rings rammed on to her fingers that they stuck out straight), "but I paraded before six girls, quite nice looking, but rather over-made-up, who went over me as if I was a prize vegetable, taking it all down on the typewriter" (at this point we passed a positively Wagnerian mountain, like a clenched fist, recently renamed Mt. Eisenhower). "These girls," she went on, "quite polite, of course, 'scar on cheek,' they said. Tap, tap, tap. I *have* a slight scar. Grey streak in hair, tap, tap, tap. . . ."

Now the landscape was redoubling its activities—even to the names—Mt. Bogart on the left, Aylmer on the right. We are following the course of the Bow River. And now, after the summer resort of Banff and Lake Louise, we are suddenly (in an arch of wooden art-lettering beside the railway) at the GREAT DIVIDE—five and a half thousand feet—ten thousand feet towering on each side of us—Kicking Horse Pass, historically discovered for the railway by Macdonald—gigantic scenery, heroic engineering feat, wild beasts the enemy of man . . . but to bring us down to earth again, a guide turns up in the observation saloon.

There is a sort of Canadian accent which is harsher and has less of the lifeblood of intonation than the least inflected American. This crop-head guide told us sourly that there were the remains of an old cement works *left*, that 4,500 moose were once seen on Louise Peak, and that we could have this book of technicolor photographs, all six of them, for one dollar fifty.

The afternoon was a matter of steeply sinking at a doddering fifteen m.p.h., balancing our way down the twelve-hour-long gorge towards the Pacific, twisting and turning three times longer than the crow flies, more and more autumn as we get down—back from December to November, November to October—poplars and birches like dabs of yellow wool mycelium, and the famous spiral tunnels to get us down a sudden fifty feet when needed.

After the Great Divide I was introduced to Rocky Mountain-ship. We had left the dry province of Alberta for the wet province of British Columbia, and could now drink (after two days) a limited selection of drink—e.g. whisky and Canada Dry. In the bar were two young Canadians who were apparently (I noticed critically) dead to nature. They read magazines while passing the highest peaks. Why? They gently let me find out. They had been hunting in Alberta. If you spend your time on the loftiest ranges, they said (as simple truth), the view from below isn't so exciting. They then let me realise that farther north only is to be found, to their taste, what seems to an Englishman the endless spaciousness, freedom, and innocence of *all* this part of Canada. Hereabouts, by their scale, it was as restricted as Ken Wood or Hampstead Pond. Even in Alberta you are limited to

five pheasants a day during season: in British Columbia to two.
... "The reason is *everybody* shoots." It began to seem as if we
were talking about Woking, or at any rate Mull. All the same, I
kept having to remind myself, though in Mull you might also
"get a couple of deer and a goat," you wouldn't also have to "be
sure there were two of you because grizzly can get very nasty."
"You don't shoot black bear, unless they're a nuisance ... but
don't try to feed them however pathetic they look, because
they've got bad manners—bad claws."

They were both flourishing G.P.s—and that was quite like
Woking. But more like British Columbia and B.C. distances
was the fact that one of them diagnosed and treated a leucæmia
last week, both had to be prepared for, and frequently did,
appendectomies, cæsarians, pylorics, and hysterectomies—"and
last month I opened a stomach because a woman had stuck a
knife up to the hilt in her husband when he was late for supper
once too often. He came home dead drunk, and when he woke
up he said, 'Where's my supper?' The husband and I had to
spend a lot of time trying to keep her out of court." At this
point the guide came and told us to look at Buzzard Gulch, but
mentioned we would get the full effect only with Wilkins's
bi-polarised sun-glasses, a dollar fifty. Two victims fell, in spite of
my murmured warning.

The *prices* on this train: gin and lime, 8s. Ordinary breakfast,
12s. 6d. One English lady is half-starving, having come from
England to spend three weeks with her daughter and new grand-
son in Vancouver. The British Government allow her £30 to
spend in Our Dominion for this occasion. I told her my views
on this; I mentioned a fact she had not thought of. She ate her
first breakfast for three days.

19th–20th *October, Vancouver*. A good place. In fact, I am
still in a glow from the beauty of the scene and from the civilisa-
tion, humanity, and friendliness of the people I met in Vancouver and Oregon.

Vancouver first. My first impressions of Canada were bad.

was alone in Winnipeg on a numb Sunday evening—the lady at the candy shop bridled as I counted my change: "I think you'll find our money decidedly more valuable than yours in America," she said. But Vancouver had this Rockies approach to raise the spirit, this progressively contrasted Wedge Fugue of depth and precipice; it had also this mighty curve of bay and isthmus and wooded island. Where had I seen it before—the clean drop of the sides of the land into the sea? Salcombe, in Devonshire; and—nice link by geology—the land here, as there, was gradually submerging. It was a "drowned" shore, meeting the risen water cleanly therefore, untattered by thousands of years of wave-nibbling.

Then there is the strange home-again feel which leap-frogs across longitudes from England to New England, to the still newer and nearer to England out here. This effect was embodied in the welcoming personality of Professor Binning, and also in the fact that he is the first Arts man I have met in North America. He is an art teacher for pleasure and an artist by pursuit, exuding the tastes and atmospheres of painting and the stimulating smells of Chinese White and Yellow Ochre, in which, for a quarter of a century, married to an artist, I lived myself.

I got my lecture over very early, at the classical hour of students' lunch-time. Sound-proof sandwiches were eaten; but this did not impair the responsiveness of students. Earle Birney introduced me (self-effacing, amusing author of *Turvey*, best-known of humorous Canadian novels).

After lecture I was allowed to go for a walk alone, in the warm sun, round the bay. It is really hot sun only in the summer. You can lie sun-burning on the grass there, and afterwards be transformed, by car and funicular, into a man on a ski slope within the hour. I know no more pleasant feeling than "Lecture Over," if I've got away with it. I can really look at things. I saw lots of that tall, vulgar, pretty, purple balsam which is now clambering everywhere on northern English river-banks. In the middle of my walk I suddenly, in park land, came on a collection of totem poles. Boring in pictures, their colours, and the texture of their cedar wood, and the abstract figures, signifying whales or crows or family histories, are delicately gaudy, and all the more cheerfully decorative because they have no connection, as I had hitherto vaguely imagined, with sadistic gods and gloomy secret religions.

It was after the lecture that the hospitality really started. First the university art gallery. Special exhibition of the work of the Los Angeles nun, Sister Mary Corita. What a show for Gimpel Fils! Like a lithograph in texture and process, though done on a material; truly serious religious themes, delicate colouring; shadowy, imaginative composition. More interesting from the Canadian point of view were paintings, retrospective, of X, an old man now, once one of "The Seven"—Canadian pioneer artists "who tried to paint Canada as it really was." In effect these pictures, of lakes, mountains, and ice, are Canada as it really wasn't—good Norman Wilkinson posters with Frank Brangwyn colours. In his later abstract phase X was vorticist, with swirling lines based on a theme—titles like Troubled Spirit. I much preferred Binning's more truly abstract abstracts.

Binning motored me over the great bridge to see the sun setting spectacularly in our teeth. He showed me the house belonging to Geoff Massey, Ray's son, wonderfully designed by him to fit a wild cliff-edge, yet modern, half the walls glass (charming note, the bath looks out on the garden; the garden looks in on the bath). A Binning dinner, where Mrs. Binning entertains and presses buttons (i.e. cooks dinner) simultaneously —going from one set of attentions to the other without a trace of flurry, or disorder of her *chic* (great North American female skill). Vancouver's nearness to the Far East rubbed in by Japanese wood plates, forks, salad bowls, etc.

This nearness further emphasised when Earle Birney took me to the Chinese quarter next evening. This visit was preceded by a fifteen-minute radio talk, a radio interview, a TV interview, and golf, at the highly scenic Capilano picture course, steeply set at the foot of mountains. Here one of my lunch hosts was Hugh Martin. I shall not forget this course, nor my host. A complete stranger hit me over the head with one of those gigantic pieces of American helpfulness which leaves one in no mood to win a golf match. I had wondered out loud to him whether I should spend spare time at (1) Beverly Hills or (2) Las Vegas and Arizona. He most fortunately persuaded me into (2). But could I make both visits in the time? Today I found he had routed me, time-tabled me, fixed every air connection, warned friends to look after me in both places, and (as a final thrust) handed me an envelope with my tickets inside. "Pay me when I next come to London," he said.

27th October. Left Vancouver by 8 a.m. train for Oregon and the U.S. again. At the station I indulged in one of my heart-attack scrabbles, because (*a*) I thought station much nearer, and (*b*) forgot I had to have passport ready. Only three minutes to find it. I tore through my luggage like a terrier forcing its way into a rabbit hole; half a dozen onlookers watching intent and unsmiling as if they were observing some aboriginal custom. In the train the peace of U.S. railways would have descended on me but for the fact that a half-empty coach was made crowded by the presence of four Chinese children, who played games all over everybody.

I only discovered the spacious dining car later. The head attendant was a Welshman who had once crossed the Goldhawk Road (Shepherd's Bush) to go to the Green Man, ten minutes from my own London home. This was 1940, and when he came back he found house, wife, and children destroyed by a bomb. His life stopped; but he sealed off the tragedy, cut clear and made a success of a new start in Oregon—"I never think of it except when I meet someone like you." Chinese children get more and more worked up. Their great-grandfathers were imported as coolies to help finish the Pacific end of the C.P.R. We are along coastline most of way. The fringes of the water are choked with a plague of little birds sitting on the sea and up-ending every five seconds for food. They are migrating south. What seagull has slaty top-half of head? Must bring bird-books next time. Autumn is gradually getting younger again, as I migrate in the same direction as the birds.

The reverend seniors of U.S. are the engine drivers and conductors of these main trains, all old and benign, lined, silver hair: like stage archdeacons. Seattle a less-so Vancouver? I am more than ever, now, in the country of WOOD—rafts of it, chips of it, bonfires of waste wood, barges piled to a pyramid with sawdust, barked trees, square logs, log-mill companies; the Cavanagh Lumber Transport Co. advertises ONE PIECE OR A TRUCKLOAD.

Portland—the Multimill Hotel. Expensive as hell, no doubt. I was called for and driven to Reed College for dinner with the urbane and impressive President. I was tired, and though the food was perfect, à l'Américaine, the salad to begin with, like the pudding cake at the end, was so sweet that it dried my mouth up as if it had been bitter. The lecture hall was only five-sixths full: the mike was hanging in the worst position, above my head, so that when I wanted to get that intimate close effect I had to stretch my neck towards the top of the roof like a dog howling.

It went pretty well: afterwards the students revived and eased me with their quick amusing talk. As a matter of fact, the ice was broken fairly near the beginning of my speech. I forgot a new lecture rule I had learned, namely: "If you see an opportunity of bringing in some graceful local reference or complimenting your audience on their world-wide fame for whatever it is, DON'T DO IT." Most audiences hear the self-starter for that kind of effort growling away long before the engine is firing, although they may put on a pleased expression so as not to disappoint a lecturer obviously delighted with his deft little touch. To my amazement I heard myself chuff-chuffing into a monumental deftness tonight, all sirens blowing, and it got the biggest laugh of the evening, unintended by me. I said (on later history of English humour), "Our *Punch*, like Reed College, was once highly progressive. Later it became pompous."

I make a recording; then there is a reception, then kind hands waft me on way. The MacRaes (Literature) take me to the Garlans (Philosophy), where I meet also the Tuhys (Medicine). They are highly read in gamesmanship, and try to put me off by a series of admirable ploys. Dr. Tuhy has the quiet, matt, quick American voice, a sort of cross between Joe and Bob Hope. We were laughing till 3 a.m., all thoughts of that parching sweet jelly and my foolish lecture to a shrewd but kind audience forgotten.

22nd October. I had to decide today whether (*a*) to rush to San Francisco and back, or (*b*) get to know Oregon better. I am glad I concentrated on Oregon. When the New England population were getting overcrowded a hundred years ago they discovered their own weather, plants, waterfronts and skies duplicated in this other, emptier Eden in the top left-hand corner of the States: only more of everything. The English were finding it, too, but the Americans did it more pushfully.

I half-liked geography even when it was a map on a foggy schoolroom wall. I love it when the country itself is your map. There is an enormous bas-relief, physical map of the States which I would give anything (but not quite $40) to have. It is in Matson's office. The mountains, the plains and the river-basins are beautifully clear. It explains the history of the States. How the first Eastern States were bound to be the first to be settled. What a big jump it was across the Alleghanies. Why New Orleans had to happen, and why St. Louis, at the centre of all river-systems, was preordained. It also explains the wonderful courage and heroic travelling, brilliance and technical skill of the first finders of the trails across the Rockies, which—and it's so difficult to fix that in one's head—stretch, except in the north, half-way across America. It shows also how the west coast was an El Dorado: it shows the gods' gift of the peculiar, fertile, symmetrically oval Sacramento Valley: it shows how the plains and harbours in Oregon and Washington seem created by God for Man (English-speaking, of course).

The Oregonians are highly aware of all this and make a point of remembering that they are at the goal end of the Oregon Trail, only one or two generations removed from settlers. They are wild-beauty-conscious and civilisation-conscious simultaneously.

The Garlans drove me along the Oregon Trail by the side of the Columbia River, one hour to the country-place of the Tuhys. The trail is now two first-class roads, each with a wide double track of traffic. The Columbia Gorge is on the mile-wide, mile-high scale; Mt. Hood, with a splendid and permanent head of snow on it, presiding in the distance. The gorge is not made less wild by "This Is Wild" notices in stylised wood, meant to suggest torn-off pieces of bark, saying that we are NOW ENTERING THE SCENIC SECTION. There are high feathery waterfalls on the right of us every five miles, some with romantic Indian names, or charming English ones, like Bridal Veil. Nor is the romance of such names affected by such notices as "The Bridal Veil Reconstruction Corp" or "Bridal Veil Glue Works." Tuhy is waiting for us by the summer lake and packing an engine on to a little boat which takes us very briskly to his lakeside luxury hut which has of course the standard super bathroom and kitchen which are everywhere. Lots of Tuhy children and a magnificent sunset, but the end of the season is near and it's getting a bit cold, so that their shrieks and yells sound thin and echo-y. Most of the lakeside houses are deserted now and it's pretty dark. I had asked to be taken to the Columbia Gorge Hotel they recommended, so that I could work and write tomorrow. But it was a gambit, a trap, turning out to be the Gorge Hotel for Elderly People and Hopeless Invalids, which meant of course that I had to go back and stay with the Garlans and dine splendidly with some people called Lally. There was an American Professor of Philosophy from Cambridge here, and they hoped I would be able to out-gambit him. They wanted me to do Oxfordship against him, but I lost because he cleverly kept the talk to his own subject, which of course was fatal for me. "How can a School of Philosophy flourish without at least one neo-Hegelian?" etc. I can't keep that up for long. I had to take refuge in Another Subject; and very fortunately here my host turned out to be the first and only *plant* man I met in the States. England is riddled with nice old vicars and go-ahead young bird watchers ready for natural history chatter. Not so the States. However, Lally had all the plant books, grew wild flowers in his greenhouse and unusual conifers in his garden, told me that Oregon was particularly good for flowers because of variations in height, and that the flora was 3,000 species plus—which at least equals the whole flora of Britain, in numbers.

23rd October. Sleep at Garlans'. Woken up by Judy the daughter and Jessie the dog. It's a small house, on a professor's salary; but it's an American salary. All normal requirements on two floors, but vast spaces are dedicated to the children—a gigantic boxroom and the whole basement as playrooms, in which they constantly build towers and fall off them. Edwin Garlan has the slow, clear speech of someone accustomed to the gentle and patient explanation of philosophy. The kitchen has that marvellous oven which starts cooking at the correct moment whether one is in the house or not. Mrs. G. makes the waffles in an electric mixer in one minute. I have orange-juice and bacon and egg, the bacon, as always, in rashers of identical thinness, shape and saltness and texture—same all over U.S. and exactly right. They have two second-hand cars, regarded as "ancient" because three years old. One they lent to me to drive off for the day. I am very gingerly with my first experience of left-hand drive. It is unexpectedly difficult to judge right-wing clearance. I often at first crashed lights, as I've conditioned myself to traffic lights placed in a totally different position. I find the multiplicity of notices confusing—it's all like having to drive while threading a needle and reading a book at the same time. Back at Garlans' we go to a fine cocktail party, lasting from six to ten, where the Tuhys' little girl, in full ballet costume, is at last persuaded to dance to gramophone excerpts from *Swan Lake*. She begins by dancing with her hand over her eyes, to make herself invisible. But once she is well started she simply will not stop, and dances beautifully in and out between people's feet for the rest of the party; and the last thing I saw, when the guests had almost all gone, was her still dancing, by herself, over imaginary feet.

There is a decent grand piano which I can't help touching; whereupon I have to play a one-finger duet with daughter No. 2, with the Tuhys' flash-bulb cameras trained on this spectacle; and now I am identified as one of those miraculous people who can play the piano. Again, this U.S. perceptiveness—they will listen to me on the piano. Suddenly a volume of Gilbert and Sullivan is placed before me. Well, when the Tuhys come to stay with us, as I hope they will, I shall leave a volume of Longfellow on the spare room bedside table. "English music" (and this with us now is England's second golden age) means so often in America either Sullivan or Quilter. They even allowed me afterwards and encouraged me to play the piano score of *Oklahoma* in my hideously unrhythmic way, which seemed to them another sort of miracle. Most of them had excellent voices and sang "White Sands and Grey Sands" for about an hour. Nothing expresses the lopsidedness of American education so clearly as the fact that these philosophically and bookishly educated people, sophisticated in conversation and brimful of potential music also, continue to aim their musical sights surprisingly low. I like Sullivan, but the Sullivan opera books here do not contain his pretty accompaniments, only a kind of four-square arrangement of hymn-tune chords.

24th October. In spite of the long walk and perhaps because of another party last night, I am not internally perfect. (I was perfectly "well" all through this trip, but hardly ever got the luxurious feeling of absolute *wellness*. Oregon was an exception, but elsewhere the warmed-up hotels ... the determination not to play more than nine holes of golf ... the frightful irregularity of American meals . . . the American habit of drinking fairly furiously for an hour on an empty stomach ... the searing dryness of the martinis . . . the lack of exercise-consciousness in

American males. They are much more diet-conscious than exercise-conscious here. Diet seems to be aimed at vitamin intake, and they eat such enormous quantities, such large helpings, that there must be ten times more vitamins in a single meal than are necessary to last them for a whole month.)

We have this small business of electing local lifemanship officers. I asked Mrs. Garlan to lunch, so that by special arrangement she, as Oregon (East) One, could re-establish her One-upness over Mrs. Tuhy—Oregon (West) One. This is my neat way out of the lifemanship gambit plotted against me by these two families—forcing me to choose which to make Chief Gameslife of Oregon. I asked Mrs. G. to the "Stirrup Room," mentioned in *Holiday's* lists of good restaurants, at the Mult-nomah Hotel. The name "Stirrup Room" is written up in pieces of small rope to give the atmosphere of lumber camp de luxe. It is full of dark nooks like a cabin. The tables are beautiful, polished maple, or perhaps myrtle. Baked Columbia River salmon was served with a fine salad, but also with baked beans in a thick brown sauce, strangely inhibiting the salmon flavour. I realise once more, here, that one sees at least as many domesticated and happy couples in America as in any other country. I suppose it is always more so in this respect for every country than it seems from outside. Across the Atlantic one thinks of the Americans as spending half their time in Reno.

Farewell Portland, but not Oregon, for my next stop is Eugene. I move south again on the North Pacific Railway. These trains again—how calm and peaceful. Cartons for water in every coach. First-aid kit. Gents' smoking-room. Lounge-bar. Man selling drinks including milk in a carton. Sometimes it is really a blessing over here—the confidence in the cleanness of everything you eat and drink. Perfectly dusted surfaces every-where. Passengers hang their jackets and coats from hangers in cellophane covers. Diesel engines clean as a watch: shining chromium luggage van. America puts this cleanness across so forcefully that one begins to feel, apologetically, that in Britain everything is an inch thick in some sort of deposit. Yet there are, I suppose, plague- and cholera-free areas even in one's own home.

A young Eugene student sits by me, his clear young face clouded as if by impending disaster or the loss of a friend. I soon find it is the former—he is under an obligation to read a book. On his knee lies *The Return of the Native*. For a time he broods over page 2. He brightens up when I tell him I have played golf on the heath the description of which he is now reading (Egdon). He has read *Tess of the D'Urbervilles* which he pronounces "dour". He is wistfully conscious that "in Europe they are better educated at the end of High School. We sometimes can't just write a grammatical sentence." He said Reed College, which I've just left, was best at studies and therefore stood below Willamett and the University of Oregon. These rank high he said because they are more social. He begins to expand this theme richly. "The University of Portland (Eugene) is a sort of playground," he said. Eugene is my stop. It's extraordinary that I've never heard of it before; for I find among other things that it's the chief lumber city in the world.

After good cutlets at Eugene Hotel, it all starts again. I am called for by Robert D. Horn, the English professor here. He takes me up, for a drink and talk, to his country-farmhouse-looking home, built seventy-two years ago, as old as Eugene itself. He is small and sparkling, and I soon discover what his prime delightful gambit is. It is to live in this lumber world at the end of the Oregon Trail, up to his neck in shavings, as it were—and to be more knowledgeably penetrating about eighteenth-century English literature than Professor Nichol Smith himself. I began talking somehow about bad poems and quoted "Think of Three hundred Gentlemen at least," written in 1704 in honour of Blenheim:

> And each one mounted on his capering beast
> Into the Danube they were flung in shoals.

Horn: "Yes, I know—delightful. As a matter of fact, you're misquoting it."

"But, I think I got it out of Macaulay."

"He misquotes it, too, but in a different way."

"But what do you mean? How do you know? Does anybody know who wrote it?"

"Well, yes."

I didn't know anyone knew the author—much less had seen the original. Dr. Horn explained, very apologetic about having to put me right.

"As a matter of fact, I was very fortunate. I managed to get strong circumstantial evidence of the author, and years later I was able to find a copy of the actual poem. I think it's the only one in existence. I'll find it for you in a moment."

One would have to come to the end of the Oregon Trail to find this. Bundled up in his untidy study he had a first of (could it have been?) Pope's *Pastorals* tucked under a typewriter, a second of *Robinson Crusoe*. Among the cooking recipe books *Copperfield* and *Vanity Fair* in the original monthly copies looking as fresh and green as if they'd just been laid out on a bookstall. To quieten me Mrs. Horn gave me the best tea I'd yet had in America. He also had a fine set of "Occasional Poems," surely an excellent and witty choice of theme on which to base a collection. He had also, like many Americans, a passion, soaked in no doubt from the Red Indians at the end of the Trail, for scalp-hunting. But his scalps were such things as a stone from Blenheim, a blitz-burned piece of wood from Dr. Johnson's house, a shell from Pope's grotto.

25th October. Still with Horn, but this time it is a tour of wood-shavings and not first editions. He takes me to a lumber mill, the Solbeck Logging Company. Years before I had seen the majestic sight of big trees being tossed about as if they were matches in the George Lansbury mill, long since blitzed, at Bow. Here it was all on the Oregon scale. Three enclosed factories, each the size of Earl's Court, one for paper, one for reducing the biggest Douglas fir in the world to thin planks, one a railway station for packing and delivery. Everybody except us, including our guide, was wearing a crash-helmet. "When I tell you to stick close to me, you must keep practically touching me," he said. Enthusiastic and jolly, the guide was able to make his voice audible through sound which suggested giants playing with fire-irons and coal-scuttles. Enormous tree-trunks are fished out of a dirty artificial lake and come up to Stage One on an escalator. Stage One peels off the bark with jets of compressed water sharp as steel poignards, capable of penetrating clean through your hand. Then the logs are ready for their first rough shaping into four-corneredness and thick planks. Typical of America—there are notices helpfully telling you what it's all about. While terrifying iron arms lift the logs into position, the carving up is done by a machine (see notice-board) called a "PONY RIG . . . HOW VERSATILE IS THIS MACHINE . . . A SORT OF COMBINATION EDGER, U SAW, AND BED RIG." This appears to be one man in a shunting engine fitted with fifty steel hands, capable of twenty changes of direction, darting about on rails, sawing through logs as if they were the consistency of chocolate fudge, while two attendant men, nimbly and dangerously, catch the foot-thick sections as they peel off, and guide them on to the next process. "In a year's cutting we could build 12,500 wooden houses."

Horn shouted to me, through a clatter so loud it must have had weight and shape, to tell me he still had, somewhere, a first edition of the *Sentimental Journey*.

Our guide likes to make jokes. He paused before a hundred-foot ladder leading to the top of the shed as if we were supposed to climb it. Pausing before the delivery shed built round a rail-way siding and clamouring with different kinds of deafening sounds and the voices of a hundred packers, he says to the door-man, "Anybody at home?"

"Trucks" (i.e. goods trucks) "are the bottleneck. The South-ern Pacific want to run this country. This shed is nine hundred feet long." The guide had planted a sapling, the only living tree in sight in this desert of factory and slaughtered remains of forest.

A notice: NUMBER OF ACCIDENT-FREE DAYS. DAY SHIFT 755. EVENING 725. GRAVEYARD (NIGHT SHIFT) 50. The danger, apparently, is getting sleepy. There is a wonderful machine for replacing a knot in sheetwood for three-ply. The action involved in this quickly becomes mechanical: a nod or even a yawn may mean a lost finger.

The "cool-deck" is where the lumber is stacked and stored "to cool off"—i.e. mature. The Campbells came here because they thought it looked like the hills of Scotland. Most of the hills in the neighbourhood have been "pretty well logged off." One such is called "Baldy." The men who prepare the trees for cutting are called loggers ("lumberjack" is NOT an O.K. word). These men are small, sinewy, tough, and are able to hang on to the top, the thin pinnacle, of a gigantic fir, which catapults fifty feet after they have cut one of the branches off. There is a logger fatality every week—one yesterday. Nine years ago this place was a barley field.

Another U.S. characteristic, besides bigness of scale, has manifested itself in Oregon. Both the foreman and Horn were expert and sensitive guides. The point is that in the U.S. they like showing you round. We in G.B. don't. I tell Horn that when he comes to the Lakes someone will say, "Dove Cottage? Somewhere up there. Ask at the Post Office." Horn agrees. He said: "When I saw the Queen's Doll's House at Wembley there was some sort of man in uniform who kept saying, 'Don't hang about there, please.' We were in a queue and we don't like standing in queues. We won't wait to be served in shops either while the girl rearranges the stock or tidies her hair." There seems to be a third characteristic covert in this comment. The English are relaxed and content, standing in line for things. The shuffle forward, every minute or two, gives them a sense of progress.

After all this I had to start the singing for my supper.

Sometimes I enjoy this as much as I enjoy the travel and entertainment. This was one of those occasions. There was a lunch
at the Faculty. Then I answered their questions for fifteen minutes. Then I talked for fifty minutes to another bunch of the best
and liveliest students—the sort of audience that a more or less
comic, semi-amateur actor like myself prays for. Then an
unscripted half-hour's brains trust for a C.B.C. hook-up,
with myself doing most of the talking. Then "informally asking
questions during tea for anybody who cares to come in" (there
were about seventy, including those standing at the back). All
the time the wonderful Horn was in the background helping
to make things go—and, un-donlike, helping to make the radio
interview go by his wit and self-possession.

A pleasant comedy character made intermittent appearances
during the day. He was a charming Swedish student studying
journalism here; and his "practical" was to interview me. But
he was as yet so untrained in ruthlessness, he was still so haunted
by the Swedish tradition of good manners, that in spite of all
the opportunities and help we could give him, he could never
decide what questions to ask me, nor bring himself to ask them
when he had. And he was so self-conscious about the bad form of
putting things down in his notebook that he almost tied his arms
into a bow-knot trying to write the stuff down behind his back.

I leave Oregon with deep regrets. Plane to Sacramento—
California the Golden at last. Met at the airport by my host and
a friend, both zoologists, who drove me off in a really silky
Buick to my hotel.

26th October. I am more or less on my own till this evening.
In a motel—El Rancho Sacramento. Might have got up very
early to fly for a long midday to San Francisco, the proximity of
which fills me with vague longings. Instead I stop here and study
the motel and go for a walk. The sun was warm and cool. I
could almost sit without shirt. The palms bursting with health—
not like those miserable stick-in-the-muds we try to grow on
the south coast. There are wide roads between the lines of

one-storeyed motel rooms, low, ranch-type, with Italian tiled roofs and half-size, Disneyland lamp-posts. There are a dozen motels almost in view. They make the longed-for contrast with the vast prison-houses of the main Cleveland-Chicago hotels. TV, bath, and shower in the one room, two settees which swivel and transmigrate into one double or two single beds, a heated swimming bath and Ed Somebody's Band in the room adjoining the big restaurant, where you can tea-dance and supper-dance. Complete bookstall, minor drugstore, etc. Longing to motor across the States using these.

On my walk along the main road I run into a section displaying caravans. They are on show out of doors, but remain much cleaner and brighter in this air than if they were in a London shop. They are long, gleaming things in stainless steel. Not only are they much more sensibly decorated than their English counterparts—i.e. with very few, if any, bijou knick-knacks; they are more comfortable and the more luxurious, pullman type, 6,500-dollar ones somehow manage to include a reasonably roomy double bedroom, another bedroom with two singles, a sitting-room, bath and shower and wash-basin, a kitchen with all the gadgets, and swarms of electric lights. The big customers for these are retired couples who live in them all the year round, migrating by the season.

I increasingly find it easy to imagine the advantages of side-stepping the thermostatic difficulties of older age, and living, as one can live in this country, in a permanent temperature of early June. I walked through the fringes of the town. The species of thirty weeds were all unknown to me, though the genera mostly familiar. Only the tender and trivial but, Euphorbia-like, completely irrepressible Petty Spurge was English.

On the way I stepped for a hamburger into the dark bar owned by Jerry Grieffspar, the Well-Come Inn on Davis Highway, Sacramento. I started wanting to talk to him when this enormous ex-boxer, asked by a customer if he'd "seen my boy play in the school game yesterday," cleared his throat and said, "Yes, I caught a glimpse of him." This obvious white lie, for politeness's sake, revealed that he was human. He showed me all his photographs, all pasted on the wall, one taken with Tommy Farr. Here you can get beans for forty cents, T-bone steak for $1.85, cheeslings with french fry for ninety cents. On the wall is written: THE LOUDER YOU ARE TONIGHT THE QUIETER YOU WILL BE TOMORROW. I HAVE NO CREDIT, NEITHER HAVE YOU.

At the post office I sent off some books. The two girls there told me exactly how to do it, both talking at once. "How have you enjoyed it?" they asked.

"I like it here."

"That's what we want you to say."

Dr. Salt comes to give me dinner at El Rancho. Californian Riesling is perfectly all right. The lecture here at Davis College could never have been one of the hundred-per-cent ones. This is the agricultural college of the great university—"The Farm" they call themselves. A 450 auditorium almost full and the audience laughed—often only out of kindness to me because they couldn't possibly have got more than half my stupidly abstruse references. Pleasant party afterwards, mixed. After it was over I inspected one of those domestic electric organs, played very well by my host. Bach was scarcely known to him, and what he played, with extraordinary self-taught skill, were gentle pieces of the "Grey Eyes Across the Sunset" order. Pronunciation note for English visitors: Mizzouri. Arkansaw, but the Arkansas River. Most teachers passionately agree with me about scholastic backwardness of pupils when they arrive. Democracy points. *One:* College girls do baby-watching to ease finance. *Two:* Dr. Salt said he only knew golf "as a caddie": which he was for two years at week-ends as a boy for dollars. In England this would permanently endanger his amateur status.

Wonderful post from England today; cheers me up just at the right moment—at my most distant point from S.W.1.

* * * *

I am glad of this coming little holiday, a break from lecturing. Sometimes I rather curse the day that humour was chosen as part of my theme, and the word seems to hang around like a spectre. On the wall behind the platform I seem to see HUMOR written in iron letters, and I think of it as I approach the forbidding hotel or the neo-Gothic campus.

But, in fact, on this tour I have tried for the first time the technique of more or less repeating the same lecture, and to my surprise I have found it a real way to learn and to improve. Instead of the lecture getting staler, it gets fresher. It feels like this: as if I am first roughing the material, then moulding, then polishing, as I stand on successive platforms. And this material is not lecture but audience.

The first time I give the lecture I make a mental note of the bits which have given the audience that dead, blank, puzzled look— which reflects the blank, bookish, infertile parts of my lecture. They bounce straight back at me. Gradually receiver (audience) must become as active as giver—in fact receiver gives back in the form of laughs, or alert silences, or changes of expression. The laughs, particularly for a speaker like me, put me in shape, and are a "give" which makes me give. About one-twentieth as well as a good actor or comedian, I can "play" the laughs. It is like moulding the cream on the top of the cake with your finger.

For instance, in one section I discuss the Potter-Ustinov collection of theatrical clichés. It runs like this. I say: "You know the kind of remark which is made in the theatre but never in life. Could never possibly be made in life. Well, of course, I absolutely love some of these. There comes a time, usually about half-way through the second act of a play written —perhaps—by a woman dramatist, when the wife says to the husband: 'Oh, my dear, if only I'd understood.'"

Now, the audience never get the hang of this first example; and it is important that there should *not* be a ready laugh here, otherwise the big laugh won't come where I want it. So I go straight into Example Two:

"John, do you think it's going to be all right . . . about us, I mean?"

I don't wait for any response to this, but suddenly say loudly and explosively:

"Oh God, Mary, what a blind fool I've been all along."

If I follow this order and timing, I invariably get one of those grand, ear-filling laughs. Any other sequence fails. Another point: the response is equally quick to one more good example ("You were always the lucky one, Gerald," etc.). If I try a third (which tempts me because I like it), there is only a half-strength laugh. Now this is bad, because half-strength after whole-strength means that laugh-saturation-point has been reached, and it is time to change the mood to something serious or informative.

I have to keep reminding myself that an audience is not individuals, but a unit. Try addressing your remarks to one person only, or even one row in the audience, and watch the audience collapsing, like peas running out of a hole in a bag.

"Getting" the audience at the start—that is to say, making this compound entity, self and audience, one—can be I believe largely a question of more or less conscious tricks. I have often seen lecturers start with a complacent "It's all right, audience: I'm one of you really." They make some self-derogatory remark, or obviously phoney boast, in the first half-minute.

It is two-thirds of the way through a lecture that the sog period comes and contact may go. The great thing here is for the lecturer to try to make himself believe that he is revealing something tremendously important at that moment; and if what he is saying is, in fact, padding and dished-up old facts from a textbook, he must speak it as if practically every word is as positive as it is profound. If it is some dead phrase like "basic difference," they say the word "basic" with a slight pause before it as if it had never been used before.

*   *   *   *

27th October. Leave Sacramento 8.40, arrive San Francisco 9.20. Perfect view, flying, of the Golden Bowl of the Sacramento

Valley—in shape might be the Weald. I have two hours to taxi round with a driver who is so enthusiastic about his town that he spills description and facts faster than I can take them in.

He first shows me the big new Freeway (autobahn) and the side of the hill which is being scooped out to straighten it and replaced across a corner of the harbour. Then he goes into a rhapsody of biggest-in-the-worldness. There two miles away is the largest aircraft carrier in the world, the *Forrestal*—there is the largest dry-dock in the world straddled by the largest crane in the world. This is a frightening six hundred feet wide and a hundred and fifty feet high. Nearby is a sub-chorus of cruisers, battleships, and a largest hospital ship. But I still think of the *New Yorker* drawing caption: "All right, you've made the biggest hamburger sandwich in the world. So now what?" It is, in fact, the lack of the bigness complex in San Francisco itself which makes us—and many Americans—love it.

Lines of city blocks are being removed for the new Freeway, so that the last five miles of this road will cost one and a half million dollars a mile just for the property. Hence the petrol tax has been increased by thirteen cents. But in California all money taken in petrol tax goes to local highways except for six cents, and even that goes to Federal highways within the State. Poor England, misusing her Road Tax, soon to be bottlenecked to immobility! Then there is the exact length of the San Francisco bridge, a real biggest in the world. The fogs are another "biggest" and something to be proud of. He describes the mechanism of the hot air sucked from the heat of the Sacramento Valley and turned into fog against the windscreen of a coast range cooled by the tail end of the Japanese current which makes the sea here too frosty for the unhardy Americans to bathe—a Gulf Stream in reverse.

The *centre de ville* buildings ... the plain Opera House, which my guide doesn't say is the biggest in the world, but it has "the finest acoustic this side of La Scala" (pronounced "Scale-a"). He shows me Van Ess Avenue, wide because two streets were blown up to break the fire after the 1906 earthquake. He, too, likes the un-American lack of height in the buildings, and calls it the best real big small city. Chinatown is Chinese to the eyebrows in a film-set way. Even the traffic-lights have Chinese lanterns as finials. WELCOME TO THE WORLD'S LARGEST CHINATOWN. It's funny to see a concrete block of council flats decorated with Chinese ornaments and lettering. We go up, of course, to Telegraph Hill, and I stare and stare at Alcatraz Island, frightening because of the great sunshine and because there is no sign of people. Only the prison. Then we go down to the expensive Marine Boulevard with its mixed Hollywood architecture, including concrete reproductions of French villas and Tudor cottages and modern buildings, all mixed up. All very expensive, yet they could be bought for a song in 1944 because the inhabitants, calling it Burma Road, left in a body since for some reason they thought it was the ideal target for Japanese bombers. Nearby is the fantastic, super-Corinthian Parthenon left over from the World Fair, 1915, and decaying in gentle chocolate colours half-curtained with vegetation, like a discarded film-set on the fringes of a film lot—a very American kind of ancientness.

It was a bit of a rush back to get my plane for Las Vegas. This was my finest air journey. First the coast range, then the Sacramento Valley, then the Sierras, peaks in a sort of regularity of roughness, as monotonous and unplanted as the sea. Mt. Whitney, highest in America, scarcely stands out. Then Death Valley and other dead, flat-bottomed arenas, like worn-out pitches in the deserted playground of giants. Yet there are isolated houses, roads like lines drawn with a thin stick in sand, and even little settlements.

Las Vegas itself is a circle of mountains, the colour of smoky red sunset, linking arms round a flat plain, and one only has to step outside into the desert to feel that this comic little hell of time-wasting and gloomy hypnotised squint-brains (or gorgeously amusing place full of real *people*, my dear—whichever way you look at it) is laid bare under the eye of a sarcastic God.

On Hugh Martin's instructions I go to the Desert Inn, one of twenty-five such on the long "Strip." These gambling hotels are on the motel principle, only more so. They are cheap for what you get, including, e.g., superb floorshows for the price of a drink, and beautifully designed swimming-pool at normal Grade One hotel prices.

Obviously therefore the Las Vegas gambit is to go there and not gamble. I started by trying another gambit—which was to walk into the middle of the desert and pick three flower specimens, since obviously no one has ever done that at Las Vegas before. But though I did, in fact, get a very pretty little poppy made apparently of velveteen, it was no use, because nobody here takes any notice of you anyway, or any notice of anybody or anything else. All are hypnotised by a small, single-minded desire to gamble. The rather beautiful *entraineurs* and chorus ladies are scanned only perfunctorily. Breakfast is served at any hour of the unsleeping twenty-four. Meals are not regularly eaten in the restaurant except by elderly couples daringly playing truant on a golden wedding anniversary spree. The average age of customers is high. On the double row of shining slot machines which line every hotel, every shop, every bar, even the golf professional's shop, lines of elderly women pull the levers as they put in coins from a little tin can and wait for the jackpot to come out. When the jackpot does come the number of the machine is flashed in neon lights, also the words "YOUR (125TH) JACKPOT TODAY." The slot-machine odds here are better than, say, at the Chelmsford Golf Club, and in fact it took me a quarter of an hour's hard pulling, two machines at once, before I finally lost all my three dollars' worth of dimes.

Down-town, however, in the honky-tonk joints, the gambling is rather different. I don't much like gambling myself—still less do I enjoy insulting good games by introducing the money incentive. But like everybody else, I am interested in the laws of chance, and in the problem of chance itself, and the question of whether any element in life can really exist in pure separation from all will and influence. I have been concerned with two coincidences involving odds so gigantic—of the order of 100 million to one—that it is impossible not to wonder whether even chance may not be part of a pattern, or whether, alternatively, these coincidences may not be connected with some complex form of telepathy. It follows naturally, therefore, that I have been interested in the Rhine experiments, an interest whetted by a recent long article of Aldous Huxley's in which with his good scientific clarity he summarised the results and outlined future developments, an interest made a little more concrete by the fact that my last lecture of this tour was to be at Duke, the university of Dr. Rhine.

Dr. Rhine is the distinguished psychologist who has proved what has long been known empirically, that telepathy is a fact, and that certain individuals are more susceptible to this unknown force than others. More recently, with the same patience and thoroughness, the same long series of trials with volunteer helpers, he has proved equally the existence of precognition. He has demonstrated that it is possible to do better than guess, that it is possible to *anticipate*, more than fifty times out of a hundred—say fifty-three times—whether the coin will fall heads or tails. More fascinating still, it is possible to *will* a rolling coin, in about the same percentage of cases, to fall one way or the other. Some of these experiments are made with dice mechanically propelled. Would it be possible, by an effort of will . . . ? But I do not properly understand the dice game.

However, in the down-town section of Las Vegas, at the Solid Emerald, there is a machine the working of which even I can understand—a kind of huge ship's steering-wheel which revolves slowly while the spokes flip against a leather prong. The prong gradually brings the wheel to a stop. Watching it one becomes slightly hypnotised. Stuffed between the spokes there is a dollar bill or a five or a ten or a twenty. If you put your money on 20 or whatever it is and 20 comes up, you get 20 to 1.

The odds, I suppose, were arranged to be slightly worse than six to four against the backer. Still, with determination . . . supposing I wanted it to stick at 10, for instance, could I somehow put the brake on with my Rhine will-power? What *is* willing it? *Be* . . . *ten*. No good. Let me try *thinking* it more. At the second try (tens were about 17 to 1 against) it did stick. I put a quarter on the 5 to 1 mark. That would be roughly 8 to 1 against. *Mmmmm*. It stuck at 5. Then a half dollar on 5. It didn't. Then a dollar. It did. To my amusement (which of course I couldn't share—nobody *talks* to anybody in this sacred temple of chance) I found that after fifteen minutes of quite exhausting will I was 25 dollars up. How unstartling. A thousand dollars up, and somebody might have cocked one eyebrow. But 25 was quite enough to interest me. I got out into the air, to take another rubber-necking walk along the Strip. But I wanted to get back to my wheel.

I was rather tired when I did get back to my Solid Emerald. The same men were there, prospectors or miners from Death Valley, their chins that much scrubbier. I still had my five dollars intact. It would be rather good, I thought, to be able to throw off to J. or A., my sons, when I get home, that I had "cleaned up 100 dollars at the Solid Emerald." I would put my 5 fives on the fives. Five successive efforts of will, while, of course, my original stake quintupled itself. Number one—no good. Number two (big breath)—failure. Number three (I willed so hard that my teeth hurt)—failure. Four and Five were equally against me. The best part of ten pounds come and gone. It is always like that in the end, whenever I gamble. Indeed, this time it was as if fate were deliberately working against me; for I noticed one peculiar phenomenon. On three of my tries it seemed to me that the spoke of the wheel, when it appeared to be about to stop at a five, slipped past it with what might almost be described as a piece of microscopically spiteful acceleration. Slipped past it to a 10, to the great disadvantage of the management: for that was where most of the bets lay. How did this fit in with the Rhine theories? That was something I was to find out later.

28th October. There is a good, well-watered 18-hole golf-course attached to the Desert Inn, and I walked over it to examine every hole and the texture of the blue grass; and I then drove fifty balls on the driving range, getting much blessed sun and sweat on my face. Guessing one could feel pretty lonely in Las Vegas, I took an early plane to Phœnix, Arizona, over more desert mountains and the black and buried gorge of the Colorado. I saw Lake Mead in the distance, so pale a green that it seemed as if even its waters must be withered by drought.

Hugh Martin had asked Tom Darlington to meet me at Phœnix airport. I wandered about—couldn't see anybody possible; but the tough, Linklaterish-looking British colonel with a good-looking lady turned out to be Tom Darlington himself. His "meeting me" was interpreted by him as a full-scale assignment. First of all we went to the Scottsdale bar. There is supposed to be a lot of riding and rough riding round here, but in fact I saw a horse only once. They make a great point, with notices, of horses having right of way. I saw the garage opposite was called Auto-Livery Stable. We then had dinner at a show-place restaurant called Green Gables, where I saw my horse, because a knight in armour, with a sword in his hand, galloped out on a white charger to escort our car up the drive to the entrance. Attendants dressed as Robin Hood's Men let us in. Behind the bar was a panorama of a castle in three-ply, and whenever the band had to play "Happy Birthday To You," a dummy ghost appeared on a turret and the voice of the song came from its mouth. Yet the atmosphere was not strictly medieval. T. D. then took me to my room because I was dying to go to bed early after the desperate gambling of last night. This was a motel called Desert Lodge. There was a brilliant moon, and above us was a mountain called the Camel and beyond another called the Mummy, from their respective shapes. This (utterly comfortable) motel was in the desert. "Don't wander off," they said, "because of the snakes"; so I did go for a three-mile walk up towards the mountain, but kept exactly to the middle of the road. Never in my life before had anyone told me to be careful of snakes, or of any animal.

29th–30th October. These two days were the best holiday part of my tour. I twice played eighteen holes of golf with Tom on the Paradise Valley course. I've never played on a more beautiful one—the mountains so clear in this air that they seem within reach of one's arm; and the shapes of all those powerful and flourishing cactuses rising from the infertile floor of the desert. Sometimes I feel forced to make drawings, although I can only draw unskilfully.

Playing golf meant, as usual in the U.S., nine holes before lunch and nine holes after. The entrance fee to this club is $1,500, and in spite of the fact that each fairway has to be watered by a honeycomb of spouts every day to keep it to its bright, crisp green, I did wonder slightly where all the money went until they told me why the entrance fee was going *up*. The new bathing-pool in front of the club-house had been "obviously built a hundred feet too far to the right" partly obscuring a view of the eighteenth hole. So they are going to fill it in and build it in the other place.

Things to remember are: the perfect, gentle manners of my old caddie: also one of the best of golf ploys for my book. I could call it the Desert Gambit. "If you slice the ball here" (this is the material for the dialogue) "remember that the spines of the cholla cactus go through leather like knives; and if you pull (at hole six) remember that young rattlesnakes are just as deadly as mature ones." I don't know whether this was in any way arranged. My caddie had all his forearm in a bandage. Retrieving a ball from the rough, he said, he had been bitten by a side-winder.

The country lodges here are wonderfully designed with a lot of room inside, though they look compact from without. Our host, at dinner in his sweeping Frank Lloyd Wright house, kept playing *Oklahoma* on HiFi. "What orchestration," he kept murmuring; it was—but within such diffident, humble, and conventionall imits. The harmony basically Haydn, and five hundred times less advanced than Bach.

A peculiar and idiotic conversation—reminding me, for the second time, of the hopeless idiocy of ever, ever taking a superior tone. We were given wine at dinner, and I said that some of the Californian wine was really quite good. This started off Dr. K., loyally appreciative of Arizona and most things west of it. What he said in effect was that this Californian wine, a sort of claret, was absolutely as good as French wines and that all this business about French wine was a lot of snobbery. I really began to answer back at this, trying to bring into action, with a great deal of puffing and blowing, a quite unnecessarily heavy gun, looking as solemn as Abimelech.

"You have so much to be proud of," I began. "Don't spoil it——"

"How's that again?" he said.

"There is so much that is good in America. . . . Now this Californian. Amusing that it should be called 'Riesling'—it's perfectly drinkable. But——"

"Of course it's drinkable."

"That is a technical phrase we use, meaning it's pleasant."

"I'm glad to hear that," said Dr. K. Out of hospitality Mrs. K. backed me up. "What Mr. Potter is saying, Harry, is that wine in France is an ancient art."

"I know that's a very brilliant line of talk—but do you realise how long it's being going on here?"

"Not so long, Dr. K.," I said, getting a bit full in the face.

"Well, just prove it to me," he said. How does one prove it? But if anybody won, in this conversation, it certainly wasn't me.

Frequently on this tour I see places—sights—which I know I shall be able to conjure up for the rest of my life. After our golf Tom drove us an hour out into the wilderness to show me "the real desert." (Desert which has never been cleared has a different and much loftier flora.) The famous saguaros (which appear in every travel poster) grow here so tall and regularly they seem to have been planted in lines, and with their semaphore arms they must have been stared at with horror by explorers mad with thirst. Right up under wild Pinnacle Peak we went, and there, needless to say, we were not mad with thirst for very long, because Tom turned a corner and revealed his own utterly desolate and isolated cabin, luxury fitted, with a gleaming aluminium gate and a cock-tail outfit and snack-bar, and he was making and producing icy Tom Collinses and dealing out smoked salmon within four minutes.

The good thing about Tom is that without much scientific training he is one of nature's naturalists. To such people the desert is a salve and companion. He loves the cactuses, knows them all by their special names, shows me the architecture of the fibre, so light yet strong, and the extraordinary counterbalancing arms and legs put out by the saguaros if they grow lop-sided. Also the little hole near the top of the saguaros, pecked by a cactus woodpecker and inhabited either by a cactus wren or a cactus owl. The one or two saguaros on the golf-course were pit-marked by golf-balls permanently embedded in them, presenting golfers, surely, with what must be the worst lie in the world.

Tom showed me a yucca in flower, the cindery and dried-up-looking shrubbery of the palo verde, the beautiful cholla and stag's horn with the sun shining through their spiny hair, transforming their fearful prickles into haloes. Then the desert sunset, everything turning to brick and dusty red. It is perfect, beautiful and almost too beautifully the same, evening after evening. The average annual number of "O.K. for flying" days in Arizona is 364½.

It took me a long time, after Arizona, to get the dust out of my things and the thirst out of my throat. The air is so dry that sweat evaporates almost instantly; and on the golf-course, were there not a water fountain at every other hole, it would be mild torture. Perhaps the most beautiful sight I saw there was forty jets of water making high arcades against the sun on a golf fair-way enjoying its evening bath. It will take me a long time to forget this particular hospitality, this particular place, and the man who showed it to me.

1st November. New Orleans. I am afraid my lecture yesterday was rather a flop. I had looked forward to my third visit here, I had looked forward to re-meeting the delightful sponsor of this lecture, a lady who owns one of the most intelligently stocked bookshops in the whole of the Deep South, and presides personally with great dignity and charm in its dusty centre, a duchess of book-jackets. There was a pleasant interlude during dinner at her house—my first experience of Hallowe'en, which is kept with full ceremony by U.S. The tradition is that children ring the bell and say "Trick or Treat." If you don't give them a candy there hangs over your head this threat that they will play a nasty trick. The only nasty trick, I see from next morning's paper, was the man in North Louisiana who, after seventeen such calls, poured boiling water over two infants who made it the eighteenth. He is now locked up. It's much better to give them a candy—and I was allowed to do this. There was a sweet little girl of three dressed as a ghost. Most of them had to be pushed up to the doorway by their parents, and then they were too shy to speak.

The lecture was half university, half a Literary Society—and besides there were supposed, according to my briefing, to be "hundreds of interested townspeople." Well, it was held in the main big lecture hall of Tulane University and the hundreds didn't turn up. I was faced with a half-full auditorium. Great swathes of side-seats were completely empty. In three minutes I knew I was a dead lecturer and that therefore it was a dead audience, laced with a few supporters determined to laugh against the grain. This is where a truly experienced lecturer or actor would have known what to do—to *get* the audience. I tried being crisp, I tried relaxing all over so that my arms swung inertly against the lectern; I tried being loud, or slow, or quiet—but there, on the faces of the older people particularly, was that puzzled screwed-up look which reflects the fact that *I* am puzzled and taut. My mouth got Arizona dry.

Afterwards my gloom was dispelled by a few left-overs from the audience who were inclined to imply to hell with lectures anyway, and determined to save an evening which had started badly by taking me to the Paddock Lounge for drinks and jazz. One (Mr. Edmondson) was a thickset man from the deep country and had lots to say, but the band was going, and against the full blast of Snookums Mathews and the best Dixieland jazz in New Orleans I couldn't hear even if I put my ear right in his mouth; so he wrote down, in big round writing, this invitation (perhaps not perfectly unambiguous): "ERNIE E. EDMONDSON JR. AND ELIZABETH travelled two hundred miles to hear Steve Potter. Call on us to see Ducks, Rice, Marsh-alligators, Musk-rats and CAYUNS [the Canadian French southern sub-colony]. The Spirit of St. Louis, Crowley." He then talked with considerable scholarship about the variety of French accents in these parts. He then did a dance all by himself. We went to a honky-tonk opposite and had drinks, where a woman sang songs. She was enormous, with a fair wig. She was able to move her breasts in any direction, together or separately. Before she began a song she yelled furiously at her audience to "shut up." The audience was quite big. The sexy shows are three-quarters empty: the intelligent audience prefers Dixieland, or this—which caters for the higher brow. All of us parted with terrific handshakes. Bed 3 a.m.

1st November. I am being very slack here about seeing things and places. The wonders of Arizona are still whirling round in my head. This hotel is stuffy physically and mentally. There are always three or four business luncheons in the party rooms, and in the lobby a notice like: WELCOME TO THE ASSOCIATION OF FARMERS CO-OPERATIVE BONDED TREASURERS AND FINANCED EVEN-WAGE COMBINED SECRETARIES. Men in good suits walk about with their names in large letters on their lapels. Next morning they are all sitting in the lounge, and all asleep.

It's a fine day—like a fine September 10th, say, in England; and now a nice interlude. Golf with Mrs. Smith and Mrs. Mousted. Their husbands were to join us for the last seven holes.

Both husbands were going, by the way, to one of those very Roosevelt Hotel luncheons—this time to Vice-President Nixon, who looks handsome in a black-browed way, but whose speech (theme: There is no room for a slave state in the Americas, à propos Costa Rica) I afterwards read in detail, looking in vain for one uncolourless phrase. I gather the whole gambit was to get photographed chatting to Nixon; and special individual photographers were sent along for this purpose. We played golf at the big N.O. Country Club—wonderfully green and wooded—a park course. Even here you can move your ball to a "preferred lie" on the fairway, although the fingers of the Bermuda grass hold the ball up beautifully.

It was after the lecture that these fragile and pretty guests had been offered to me as golf opponents. Good women golfers on both sides of the Atlantic are usually fairly solid in the hip, so I asked one of them what her handicap was. "One," she breathed softly.

"We have a different way of evaluating handicaps in our country, I believe," I said. "Over with us that would mean you went round in about 73." She looked at me strangely, fluttering an eyelash. I did not understand her glance until to-day, when on this long course she went round in 73 shots exactly. The other lady, by fiddling handicaps, I beat with a perfect (and gallery) three at the 350-yard 18th. I provided some gamesmanship on request. In front of their husbands I picked up the women's golf bags, their holed putts, etc., so that the ladies could annoy their husbands by looking as if they were thinking, "If only Americans behaved like that." Mrs. S. shyly admitted later she was runner-up of the Louisiana Women's Open.

2nd November. Would have liked to play that golf again; but since the party didn't allow me to pay a penny nor give them a drink, I feel I can't accept their invitation; I am glad to accept Deirdre's suggestion to guide me through Park. (Her husband is lecturing at Tulane for one seminar on Fulbright exchange: her brother is my publisher.)

On the way to the Park I nearly get knocked down by tram. Must NOT get slack about this traffic thing here. Incidentally I now feel that U.S. are not very good drivers, but are more courteous to pedestrians than the English. Reason: there are no angry car-owners *vs.* non-car-owners camps as in England, since everybody has one. The cars here, especially the Buicks and Oldsmobiles, are heavenly comfortable and silky smooth to ride in. They mostly keep them four years, with only one set of new tyres as expenditure. That means that about £100 a year keeps them in perfect carhood.

Audubon Park, where I met Deirdre, lives up to its name by showing me an Audubon mocking-bird and scarlet cardinal. Plants: things like the hibiscus don't thrill me. "Live oaks" (ilex) grow huge, and they are prized because they grow old as well. (When the golf-club burned down they aimed their hoses at the ilex.) Much cypress. A camphor tree with little hard nuts. Magnolias in new guise as big trees with tangles of thick roots at the base: ducks on the lagoon with a definite twang in their quack, says Deirdre. I like the little mound specially built so that children can see what a hill looks like. It is cloudy and sticky-warm. Most surprising is the Louisiana tree parasite—this is a long, dirty, grey veil hanging from all the tree branches, Spanish Moss—graceful yet disfiguring, it seems to rob the trees of their essential freshness.

Deirdre is enjoying it here; both she and her husband like their university friends and like the students. She agrees strongly about their scholastic backwardness. Thinks it starts very early. They are "spoilt," in that nothing unpleasant to them must ever happen. At the kindergartens all is play-work, games-work; *no reading before the age of six or seven*. When Deirdre's little Annabel came back to an English school from America she said, "Why are there nasty *lessons*?" The big High School classes of forty or fifty proceed at the rate of the slowest pupil. No Latin, no prep, nothing hard, needing discipline, so that they never (I say) learn to learn (in this like many potentially well-equipped women in England) nor get the habit and technique of that essential skill.

August is terribly hot. Air-conditioning essential—Deirdre only has fans in her house. Insect horror—the big, fat roach, too big to squash. Warmth and responsiveness of the coloured people. The big business of baby-watching—baby-watchers have to be fetched, won't even walk two blocks. No living-in help—except negro, and then only in big, remote plantation houses. We agree also about the tendency to take sexual pleasures bleakly—the imaginative romantic side of it sometimes lost owing to too early co-ed dating. I am reminded often, here, of D. H. Lawrence's wonderful theme: "Sex In The Head."

This education—yet all these majestic man-made wonders of America. Perhaps this play-education, *doing* things, leads to the wonderful engineering virtuosity, from the kitchen oven to the Golden Gate suspension bridge—a nation of inspired Meccano workers, Leonardos of the handicrafts kindergarten class.

I saw one of these technological marvels tonight. I took the four o'clock from the fine, new, so clean N.O. station for Kansas City—my comfortable, lonely cubicle—and watched for the Mississippi at Baton Rouge. It was a bit too dark, but I did see instead a more wonderful sight. The train passed between avenues of incomprehensible shapes—tubes, spheres, thin towers spouting flame, all lit with starry lights. Piccadilly Circus and the South Bank exhibition as conceived by a Martian who had studied Corbusier—and five square miles of it, I should think. The Standard Oil refinery.

3rd November. Kansas. I spent many of the daylight hours to-day wandering round the banks of the Missouri by Kansas City, taking buses over the iron bridge, taking a back view of the wrong sides of airport and corn markets. The new bridge is still building, but the untopped piers make perching-places for a thousand pigeons and no one seems to be working very hard. Kansas is far less on the stretch, one feels, than much of America; and people are more friendly and easy-going here than anywhere else. Instead of "of course" or "certainly," everybody from the bus-driver to the President of the University says "You bet" in a casual friendly drawl. I flew in the dusk over the Kansas River, gleaming white, to Manhattan (Kansas), where there is the big State College. There I ring up Al Pugsley who is looking after me, and get tomorrow fixed.

On the *4th of November, Friday*, I start a fullish day. At 9.30 a.m. I give a fifty-minute talk introduced by the President, James McCain, to a full house of 2,000 students. This is one of the good audiences. A bad audience, and I turn into a sort of elderly Hamlet for the rest of the day. Good, and I become talkative and extrovert. I wander round the College. Then after lunch I manage to play nine holes of golf with Al, the young Military Instructor, a Colonel, and the English Professor. The gamesmanship of the course is that at every single one of the first nine holes the effect of my slice is multiplied by ten, and the ball rolls down the hill to perdition. Kansas only seemingly flat, from the air; for this old seabed of shale and shell outcrops in regular ridges like a ploughed field with furrows three miles wide. Then I change and come back to a Faculty dinner, during which I talk to most of my neighbours at once. After dinner, in courteous compliment to me, a local singer with a very fine voice bottled up his rich baritone and all his natural talents to sing restrained English songs to a piano accompaniment. The English songs (to please me) were a whole series of Quilter and Balfour Gardnerish, twentyish, quietly fairylandish, little songs about "My Fayre Mistress" or "Pixies and Fauns." This cast a most tremendous damper over everything, and of course I had to applaud each song as if it were exactly the sort of thing I had been longing for. However, Mr. McCain leant over to me and said, "The English don't really like this sort of thing, do they?" which relieved my feelings, though I couldn't answer him. After all, some English do; and Quilter is excellent, at the right moment.

I then had to address all these people, 150 of them, on a subject of my choosing. This was one of those informal "it doesn't matter what you say" chats which may kill one stone dead. I have not been so successful with audiences nearer my own age; and it was a subject I had never written or spoken about, nor is it necessarily so trivial as it sounds. The Small Differences between the U.S. and G.B. The small, the slight. Important because it is sometimes the near-samenesses which cause the big misunderstandings, just as it is certain Modern English-sounding words in Chaucer, or in French, which are the most dangerous pitfalls to the translator.

Thoughts on this subject soon assume book-length dimensions. Let us leave it at these half-dozen notes.

Language. The nearness of our two languages is a fecund source of error. When I arrived here (Kansas City) I wanted Lux to wash my nylon shirt. "Lux," I said. "Lux," I said again, louder. The girl looked at me. "What, with keys in them?" I had to write it down. But it's not only pronunciation; we can mutually get used to that. Accentuation is more difficult. I may learn to say grīmaces, not grimāces. I must learn to say *Time Māgazine,* not *Time Magazīne.* But most misleading of all is intonation. Most Englishmen speak with the front end of their linguistic apparatus forward in the head, leaving out the chest. This sounds to American ears (*a*) slightly unmanly, (*b*) decidedly "superior," (*c*) tinnily unpleasing to the ear. Our "Thanks very much" sounds like "Thenks vedy much—*boo!*"

Now, in fact this voice means neither superiority nor un-manliness. Nobody admires it æsthetically, though some English voices sound good to us. On the other hand, the terrific deep rich gravy voice full of chest, assumed by some Americans, sounds to English ears (*a*) as if the speaker were protesting his maleness, (*b*) boring or pompous, as if an attempt was being made to dress thin thoughts in a great outerworks of stupefying vowel-sounds.

In America it takes me a fortnight to accept the fact that I am a man with an accent; equally in England it is never quite accepted that the American visitor is *not* a man with a peculiar accent, with a funny way of speaking not quite right, and therefore a man who must always be spoken to very simply and clearly. Also we always feel that no man speaking English without one of the "received" accents (Oxford, County, Winchester) is perfectly acceptable socially.

Both countries disapprove, or under-estimate the pleasures, of the rival and contrasted attitudes to language. The English love to chew the juice of a word and linger over its "right" use, adding a time-dimension flavour with a glance backwards at its derivation. Americans like and admire change in language, and take pleasure in speeding up the normal processes of language change.[1]

Democratic Attitudes. Both countries feel themselves to be the more truly democratic, and both are right. "Being democratic" is a discontinuous manifestation, peculiar to certain places, states of mind, and ways of life. These do *not* coincide in the two countries.

Food. Oh G. B., do not run down U.S. food: and vice versa. There is not the faintest chance of either of our countries being described, in the judgment of history, as Good at Cooking.

Competitiveness. America has a real taste for *laissez-faire* and for allowing everybody an equal chance to get rich, however

---

[1] The two attitudes are well illustrated in *British and American English Since 1900* (Andrew Dakers), by Eric Partridge and John W. Clark. "Again, consider the case of *hamburger* from Hamburg steak (that is, ground-beef patties), which has given rise to a bizarre development. The final *-er* is probably from the analogy of *wiener, frankfurter*, etc., though it may owe something to American analogues of *bedder* or *soccer*. However that may be, the ordinary usage now is *hamburger* for the substance and *a hamburger* for a sandwich filled with a cake of the substance. All this is normal enough; the oddity enters when the word is taken (sometimes more or less seriously, perhaps, but for the most part humorously) as a compound of *ham* and *burger*, and *burger* taken to mean 'sandwich with a broiled or fried filling of any kind.' That is, *-burger* has become, in the jargon of the 'linguistic analysts,' a 'bound morpheme.' (Bound because *-burger* is not used alone.) Despite the presumably universal knowledge that there is no ham in a hamburger, we have *cheeseburger, oysterburger, lobsterburger* (but not yet, so far as I know, *lobsternewburger*, though that blend—both culinary and verbal—will surely occur to someone in the process of time), and even (to swing almost full circle) *steakburger*—where the steak is *not* ground. I should not be surprised if the use of ham as a filling in broiled sandwiches were for ever inhibited by the linguistic problem that it would obviously give rise to. This sort of thing has, even at its worst, a sort of irresponsible playfulness that is most endearing."

certainly this presupposes a very much higher than equal chance of everybody remaining poor. There is little discontent with other people's wealth. The feeling is that (but for a temporary losing run) "there go I."

Comfort. It is not effeminate to love comfort in America. The thought, genius, and appreciation which the Americans put into the idea and ideal of comfort are partly a kind of sitting down for a good relaxed rest after 200 years of claim-clearing.

Elections. The Englishman must realise (1) that the political loyalties are bound to a freemasonry of friends, not to a framework of beliefs; and that this is how it seems to work best for America. (2) If the British are surprised to see the greatest strategist of our generation turned into an elaborate simulation of folksy one-of-us, a great man tying himself into knots in order to behave like a regular fellow, he must realise, again, that politics in America has to be more democratic in the sense that the election part of it must be carried out more under the eye, and for the approval, of regular fellows in general.

Provincial. It is important for the Englishman to understand the different significance of this word in the U.S. Loyalty to one's State is sometimes more important than loyalty to the nation, particularly in the South. It is to "no mean province" rather than country that the citizen is proud of belonging. A man is provincial. Certainly: and what a province!

Anglo-American Relations. This chilling phrase is more piercingly destructive of Anglo-American relations than any other spine in the whole prickly pear.

Remember that both English and Americans are often much pleasanter in their own countries than when they visit each other's. On the other side of the Atlantic one is always being staggered by ignorance of one's native land. Hence the neurotic impulse to say "we do that much better at home."

Mutual disapproval is due to mutual ignorance. Knowledge of the history of the United States, most rewarding of subjects, is the intelligent Englishman's biggest gap.

The best and most searching criticism of G.B. is made by G.B.

The best and most searching criticism of U.S. is made by U.S.

"I believe that the truly integrated man, the *Übermensch*, the free soul, the member of the true spiritual aristocracy of the future, is the man who can fully enjoy both cricket and baseball." This saying is capable of wider application.

*   *   *   *

Well, these notes may seem thin for even the chattiest kind of talk, but to my enjoyment this very adult gathering was as responsive as a student audience; and we laughed at and with each other. Afterwards they asked questions for another quarter of an hour, and the simplest answers and questions seemed amusing. E.g. a tremendously compressed little man in the front row wanted to know rather unexpectedly "what was the chief difference between the English and American way of making love." Loud laughter. I said the English were more romantic and the Americans more hygienic. Laughter so delighted that it left me wondering whether it was Oscar Wilde or Sydney Smith we more closely resembled. I saw more of these friends at a good, long party in Al's house, which included delicious cocktail food prepared by Mrs. Al. Once again I felt sad to go, and re-lived the gloomy mystery of the fact that, presumably, I'll never see the place again. There were eight people there I would hope to see again often: yet Kansas, dead-centre of U.S.A., seems more remote than anywhere I have been. I believe this is due to the effect, on an Englishman, of being a thousand miles removed from the sea. Even in open prairie one has the occasional momentary sensation of being at the bottom of a lift-shaft.

5th November. My hotel bill for two nights was wonderfully cheap. Contrast my bill for two nights at the Magnifico Hotel, Chicago, which was exactly four times as much. I flew to Chicago in the morning and took a long taxi to this hotel recommended by Joe's friend, Gilmer. I rang Gilmer up at 1 p.m. and he arrived at three and asked for a Scotch. I think this was the only drink I was allowed to buy him. I couldn't have been in better hands for seeing Chicago, which I should have enjoyed more had I not been suddenly transported to November the withered, whereas hitherto I had mostly been in September the ameliorating. A cold, an ever colder wind blew in from the lake and Chicago seemed dreary and impersonal with its hints of poverty, backsides of old elevated railways, and the horribly expensive, impersonal luxury and untameable central-heating of my plush hotel, with its liveried servants. First of all, Gilmer showed me a few buildings. He, an architect himself, Ruskinianly criticised the Palmolive Building and all other such skyscrapers which try to look as if they were supported by their stone facing instead of by their steel skeleton. He then specially showed me something to admire, a certain early 1890 building, and I realised that Early Skyscraper was a style to be revered. He contrasted adversely the classical vagueness and hick-pleasing mosaic ceilings of the Marshall Field building. We then went to the gallery, where after long picture-starvation I was uplifted by the wonderful exhibition of Impressionists.

There was one little Derain there which I kept seeing for days afterwards in my mind. But the most valuable picture-experience on my tour I owe to the rooms devoted to twentieth-century American painting. It is so well displayed and chosen that it seemed to give shape to the miscellaneous impressions I had gained from my glimpses of these pictures in private homes and, on former visits, in the Museum of Modern Art. Another big gap in the average intelligent Englishman's appreciation of America is surely here. But it seems to me that the knowledgeable critics in London and Paris also are too one-sided in their appreciation. They are (perhaps rather patronisingly) approving of the American abstract painters; and it is true that some of them are wonderful even if one says at first "There is a Ben Nicholson" or "There is a Mondriaan," for fundamentally the abstract artists are interpreting a Western European form.

But the "realists," or semi-realistic painters, seem to be much more truly original. For the Wyeths, the Hoppers, and the great Ben Shahn school seem to have an actuality which expresses the character of America—the mixture of new ramshackle with dignified old, the existence, so difficult to describe in words, of loneliness in the midst of crowdedness.

We then went to see a married couple called Nancy and Bertram. Their house was as youthful and good-looking as themselves. In England one still has a touching faith in the sawn-off shotgun atmosphere of Chicago; but the next stage is to realise that it is a city of sensitive sophistication, particularly in the arts and in the private art collections. Bertram is himself also an architect and interior decorator and collector. How did he fix that Degas statuette lit from an invisible source? From what hidden panel is a Brahms piano and violin sonata being played? Why are the chairs (with one arm only, a novel and perfectly comfortable design) so inexplicably effective? How did he acquire the Picasso drawings and the Klee etchings and water-colours?

But they have decided that they must try to produce a little toughness in Chicago for the English visitor; so they take me first to a very peculiar, backyard, rough little joint through puddly roads which, although it is just a bar stocked with a collection of toys and dolls, gives one the impression of being a sort of changing-house of secret vice. My host was copped for speeding, but (Chicagoship) five dollars settled that. In the German quarter we have a German meal and in the Chinese quarter we have a Chinese meal. Then to a tremendously tough pub, full of Jan Steen characters watching all-in wrestling on TV. By this time I am beginning to give out; but earlier in the day I said something unguarded about the marvellousness of New Orleans jazz. Don't say that to a Chicagoan. It's like praising pretty-peeps Cornish artists to a group of old Slade students. So I had to be taken to sit for two hours at the foot of the great cornet player, with the mottled face, at the Blue-Nosed Slipper.

Sunday was colder, and I was really beginning to feel exhausted, or rather as if I could no longer react to impressions. All the same, I am most thankful I took the El with Gilmer up to Lake Forest, the elegant suburb on the lake north of Chicago. We went to the Bill Priestleys'. He also is an architect. Except for the bedrooms his long, low house contained everything in one big room. The south wall is entirely made of glass. The architectural drawing-board, the kitchen, the sitting-down place and the music-room are four separate corners round a central fireplace. We had toured so that I could be shown more examples of modern residential houses, including a Frank Lloyd Wright house of splendid sweep and curve and swathes of impressive, windowless surface. These houses certainly seem as if they'd grown up out of the ground instead of being stuck on top of it. Architecture over, Bill Priestley took his cornet, while one of the boys played boogie-woogie, and I listened to jazz of professional standard. Many Chicagoans, not only Bill Priestley but I hear also the eminent Ashcraft, played their way through college by earning jazz money in the evenings or in the vacations. They played me professional-standard recordings of Ashcraft singing jazz to his own accompaniment. There were two boys, Kenneth and Dave, who drove me back. They were learned in gamesmanship and pumped lifemanship ideas at me all the way home, particularly asking me woomanship questions. Afterwards one of the boys, Ken, got me to write him a special letter to prove to his girl that he had really met a more or less genuine author and that I called him Ken. We took about twenty-five minutes to compose this and get it exactly right, after three crossings out by me.

I enjoyed my next lecture (at Urbana), and I think it was a success. But it occurs to me that I am giving too flattering an impression, most of the time, of my audience success. Here, for instance, is a note on one of my failures.

It was in these cold northern territories at Dampersville, let us say. It was a Woman's Club. The organiser, Mrs. Halliday, had written me a delightfully helpful note. Her husband was looking forward to picking me up and driving me down. I should be quite all right, she said, with Bob.

When it came to the point, however, Bob's enthusiasm for driving me down seemed to have evaporated. "I hope you like torpedo fish," he said.

"Yes," I said.

"Because that's what you're going to eat tonight. I caught it in the lake yesterday evening. Are you a fisherman?"

"In a sense," I began. "Many of my friends——"

"If I hadn't been meeting you I should be fishing this evening as well."

I had the impression that he disliked Englishmen and non-fishermen. I noted also that he was not specially fond of lecturers, and that I was a combination of all three—"The last one that came," he said, "nobody could hear a word he said. Do you know Boulder?"

"Boulder Who?" I said.

"Much too wishy-washy. If you've really got something to say, say it."

Dinner was uneasy, and before the lecture, standing about in the porch, the only one in a dinner jacket, like a conjurer before the children's party, I met one or two of Mrs. Halliday's fellow committee members. "Poor Mrs. Halliday," one of them said, "her last lecture was only one-third full." This one didn't look as if it was going to be too full, either. And I got the impression that, from Mrs. Ross's point of view, it would be no bad thing if this lecture was a failure as well. It was not very successful.

I believe it was Mr. Halliday who gave me one of my briefest and most memorable introductions. His manner was downright. "I expect a lot of you think that the English have no sense of humour. But wait till you hear Mr. Potter." He shut his face with a snap.

Occasionally, perhaps, the I.Q. of non-university audiences is rather low. They are all "college-trained" of course, but

148

higher education seems scarcely to have cracked the surface. They asked me questions sometimes—a dozen of them once, giving me drinks at the hotel afterwards; and one of them surprised me, when Chaucer was mentioned, by suddenly reciting the first eight lines of the *Prologue* in good pronunciation. But I discovered that he had almost no idea what it meant, nor any real notion of who Chaucer was, or when he lived. I made a note afterwards of the questions they asked me and the proportion of weight attached to each. Sixty-five per cent of them were about Princess Margaret and other members of the royal family. Isn't it awful about Princess Margaret? Isn't it a shame? Do you think she really loves him? Have you really met Prince Philip? What did you talk about? I asked them why they were all so fascinated, and a girl replied with a nice lack of affectation that they'd read about princesses in fairy coaches all their lives and here was a real one. In comparison with the British royal family none of the princesses of the rest of the world counted for anything whatever. Other important questions: Can you really get enough to eat over there? Is that really a Harris tweed; can I touch it? I know I shall never be rich enough to go round the States till I'm too old to enjoy it. Do you mean to say you can get sugar all right? Isn't the Labour Party in your country finished off now? We did *Macbeth* at school. Bevan hates the U.S. My boy aged six is learning to read by TV. When the Starlight Hour comes on he says, "That's the Smoothway Razor," because he knows those letters come on the screen then. The Prince of Wales was wonderful. We don't do any French, nor any Art. Is your beer really warm? You can't ever go too fast in England—too small. Your Malcolm Campbell is wonderful. How do you mean, our steaks are big? What's it really like in Las Vegas? I'd rather go to Paris than anywhere. We all think Dampersville is dull.

8th November. I take a bus to Champaign, Illinois, for my last lecture before New York. The University of Illinois, Urbana. These buses are driven and looked after by four handsome men, and there's always some girl who sits up near the driver and chatters to him all the time without stopping, and then Freudianly leaves her purse behind on the seat. I must cut Urbana short. A huge university, 2,000 students turned up, all went well, and I met, among other delightful members of the Faculty, Mr. Arthur Bestor, the historian of education—and this reminds me of a theme.

Urbana, Illinois, is not only an impressive centre of education, it is also a great place for educational theory and the shrewd and pointed criticism of American teaching in general. What I heard and read here helped to give a little shape to my scattered opinions.

The picture of American youth which reaches us in England in reports of sensational cases and "powerful" (almost truly powerful) films like *Rebel Without a Cause* is likely to suggest a false picture, though it pays a certain tribute to the U.S. virtue of facing its own shortcomings. On the other hand, the students themselves are often pathetically conscious that although they are pleasingly uninhibited socially, mentally they have neither the tools nor the equipment. It is fascinating to realise the way in which the big change in education at the end of the nineteenth century—the new desire to introduce more "practical" subjects—was manifested in England and America in quite different ways. In England the old discipline of the classics was exchanged for the new discipline of the "modern side"—for science as taught by such great educationists as Sanderson of Oundle.

But in some American universities the new practical took on the bizarre form of the precisely vocational subject. Students were, and are, given courses in Secretaryship, in How to Display Goods in a Shop Window, in Dry Fly Fishing. Since it was generally felt that such teaching did not quite fulfil the educational theories, however pragmatic in origin, of Dewey, there was a move to introduce Breadth of Outlook in the schools. But instead of implanting this outlook by teaching students the subjects of art, philosophy, and literature, by means of which this broad outlook is attained, broad outlook itself was taught. How To Be Broad became a set subject.

And then there is this wonderful language which the teacher of teaching has to learn. Mr. Arthur Bestor and Mr. Mortimer Smith (*The Diminished Mind*) quote some fine specimens. One must be perfectly familiar with "Cultural Upset and Reintegration," "Refined Social Knowledge and Insight," "Basic Social Processes," while being at the same time especially careful not to be "Out of Step with Cultural Reality." In his *Quackery in the Public Schools* Mr. Albert Lynd prints a "Tabular Summary of Frequency of Mention of Correlation between Aspects of Teachers or Teaching and Certain Criteria of Teaching Success." Mr. Smith finds that under the heading "Desirable Personal Qualities" *Emotional Stability* includes Reserve Dignity, Non-neuroticism, Constancy, Easygoingness, Realism in Facing Life, Stable Integrated Character; *Refinement* includes Polish, Well-readness; *Buoyancy* includes Carefreeness, Articulativeness, Wittiness.

Of course it would be as ludicrously incorrect to think of any large proportion of American students as consisting of brain-softened illiterates as it would be to mourn over them as drug-ridden delinquents. America is also a country of splendidly endowed universities and of scholars who very often outrun the scholars of the Old World in the imaginative creativeness of their research and pursuit of knowledge. Still I am sure that those who wish to understand America must know a little bit about the Life-Adjustment movement as well.

From Urbana to Chicago Airport, where I had three hours, from midnight to 3 a.m., shapelessly hanging about. Theoretically the airport is at full blast for twenty-four hours of the day; but its dead hours are a sort of well-lighted hell, à la Sartre, of waste dimness and dead spirit. Also it seems to me that all the airports are under a cloud of depression owing to the frequency (one big one a week) of air accidents. A recent example is the great dynamite murder which killed forty-three and which has given every-body real horror. But apart from that, one does hear strange stories—of an air hostess who left Ambrosia Airlines because of the tendency of the pilot's four-engined aircraft to carry on with only three of them working on the "let's have a go" principle, even when the Rockies were in the offing; or of pilots who will fly sometimes after only three hours' sleep. All this sounds like wartime, not peace. There is a general feeling that the Federal authority should take charge. Compared with the trains and the cars, aircraft look much older and less well cared for.

On *November the 9th* I spent most of the time back in New York making up sleep.

On *November* 10th Dorothy Massey and Raymond ring me up and I go along to them in the evening, and we are given dinner by Tyrone Power in his flat; also present Bill Gallacher and a girl who is head of New York *Vogue* features and, crisply smart, looks and dresses the part. The flat is full of gift treasures and, unexpectedly, there, in glorious red calf, are Power's six huge folio volumes of Steevens's eighteenth-century edition of Shakespeare. Power is handsome in an Italian way: amusing light touch—the exact opposite of the tough war hero parts he plays, yet curiously enough, and going back on this again, he in fact was a tough war hero—naval.

12th *November*. This is a day I had long been looking forward to (*a*) as I shall be back in England in a week from this moment, and (*b*) because I always wanted to compare American and English football. We were picked up from the Racquets Club and driven down to Princeton for the Princeton-Yale match. First of all we had lunch at Princeton in Joe's friend's club, then we walked down to see the match from high up on the side of the Princeton Bowl, then we came back for drinks at Joe's club, the Ivy Club, and drove back in the dark.

Princeton won the match in the second half, and it was exciting because the American game and its basic rule, trying to advance ten yards in four bursts, is as easy to follow as the street plan of

New York. It was also dramatic because the hero of Princeton, Flippin, duly did his heroic stuff, made the passes necessary and overcame a twisted knee, which to the horror of Princetonians he has refused to have treated because he is a Christian Scientist.

American football is easier than Rugby for the layman to follow. There are fewer boring pauses because no scrum; and the whole thing seems, and is, briefer. But I very much miss the beauty of the rhythmic passing along the three-quarter line, and there is much less kudos (and much less scoring value) attached to the converting kick. The weather was like sunny September in England. The undergraduateness was far more marked than it is at home, at Twickenham. There are female cheer-leaders and male acrobats and processions of Princeton Band and Yale Band forming letters on the grass; and funny dressed-up tigers and bears which had to work hard and be funny all the time. All this circus part is done in rather a half-hearted way, because although these famous colleges partly invented this sort of thing, they have been imitated in a more organised way by more junior colleges, so that Yale and Princeton are in the difficult position of having to maintain their originality and uniqueness and at the same time be superior to imitations of what they invented. The best sight was not the balloons flying aloft with HATE YALE printed on them. It came in the last five minutes of the match. When Yale was certain to be beaten, everybody on the Princeton side, i.e. ten thousand people, took out their handkerchiefs and slowly waved farewell to Yale's departing chances.

Those Princeton "clubs" where we ate are unlike anything in England. One verdant and autumnal street of comfortable private-looking houses, up the hill from the stadium, reveals itself to be a street of twenty Princeton clubs, four of which are exclusive, and the rest less so. The lawn and staircases are packed with (a) the current generation, and (b) their parents and sisters. There is a constant roar of animated and jolly conversation—decidedly unlike Leander in Henley week in this respect. I do not know whether this is due to the fact that Americans in this kind of situation are jollier and more talkative than the English, or whether it is because every single man was bursting his side jacket pocket with a pint bottle of whisky, or whether these two things are related. Anyhow, the jolliness was certainly there.

13th *November*. My appetite for taking in new U.S. sights is almost as strong as ever. I was fascinated yesterday by the smooth interlacings of the New Jersey turnpike, and the stricken-dead New Jersey land through which it passed, with manure-works, tannery and glue smells, sewage disposal, rubbish dumps and general dustbin effects.

Today I took the Long Island railway to Quogue, two-thirds of the way towards the island's eastern tip. The change to country is very gradual. Ted Patrick met me in tennis clothes. This was quite a pretty torture for me (although he had warned me) because I was longing unspeakably, after two months, to play lawn tennis myself. He took me to a house belonging to the S.'s which was on the shore and again to my pain started to play in his usual permanent Sunday foursome. He had told me of this unbreakable date, which I in England would equally and unquestioningly have asked him to let me keep. In fact, I couldn't stand it and left to walk along the pale sands of the south shore among the beautiful shells and the big clam-shells (Quogue is Indian for clam), until I got right to the point from which I could get a good map-reading angle on the wide, gentle bay. All is full of the romantic sadness of End of Season. When I got back, my suede shoes caked with sand, Mrs. S. said, "Is there much tennis in England?" This was too much for me, though I knew it was only conversation and she was hospitable and sweet. I asked if I could "try your strange surface," though the court had a perfectly ordinary concrete surface. "Oh, you play?" she said. "Yes, do knock the ball." A scratch four was fixed for a few games. I said I hadn't played for about a year, which I think was what I call a completely justified lie, and when Mrs. S. played net against me, I couldn't resist trying to send rather harder shots towards her than I otherwise would. I'm bound to say she often returned them; but I'm bound to say I was on the winning side.

After drinks, back to Mrs. Ted and Ted's house—a pale, white, low, boarded gem of light and comfort and subtly suitable construction on a sand-dune overlooking the deserted beach. The rest of the day was a question of walk, and meals, and showing Ted my Clubs article, and reading, and being lent *Catcher in the Rye*,[1] and finally having a meal in the high-class bar and restaurant which had more or less "everything," and was therefore in every way unlike anything one could possibly find a quarter of a mile inland from any small seaside community in England.

16th November. My lecture at the Town Hall I was frightened of, because I had been told it would be Older People. It was pouring sub-tropically with rain, which may or may not have cut the attendance just a *shade*, but it was quite satisfactory, good response, amusing questions, and Keedick and his distinguished father turned up and would have been all by themselves a most excellent audience. I then went to Washington; plane very late because of the weather. At Washington there was an extraordinary party which Bob Richman had laid on for me. He owes his success to the fact that he is somehow able to make people believe that it is extremely important for them to turn up on some extremely insignificant occasion. Tonight I was the occasion; and yet Bob surpassed himself by getting hold of the British Ambassador and his wife, the Peruvian Ambassador, the Indian Ambassador, Walter Lippmann and a Chief Justice. Thence to the Troys', where a lone, late caller was Herblock of the *Washington Post*, far and away the best cartoonist in America. He has a mobile and sensitive face, has had very little training as an artist, and absolutely agrees with me about the lack or rather the "Press Art School" nature of what training there is among the American cartoonists as a whole. We talked for about

[1] J. D. Salinger's *Catcher in the Rye*, a subjective study of sixteen-hood, haunted me all the last days of this visit.

three hours, much of it about politics and next year's campaign.

17th November. Today was my final lecture day of the tour and a good one. After Richman had done his brilliant income-tax work for me with the Revenue Department and I had said good-bye to my nice room and large breakfast at the glorious Troys', I took the plane to North Carolina, the airport between Durham and Raleigh. Here I was met by Dr. Griffiths, whose name sounds as if he were old and learned; but he turned out to be a young man of twenty-three who started at once talking to me about the college. He was organiser of student activities at his old university—a full-time, paid job which he referred to as his ivory-tower work. With him were two pretty girls in white blazers who were part of Duke University's reception committee. On the half-hour drive to Durham he kept asking me if there were any one thing I wanted to do besides seeing the college, and I said there was only one thing I really wanted to do and that was to go for a walk in the sun, because this was my last chance probably of getting warm sun on my face or a tiny pinch of ultra-violet into my veins until about April the 25th, 1956. He was very sympathetic and understanding, but all the same, what he showed me first was so interesting that it was two and a half hours before I got my sun. First of all I had to be taken to the college and given lunch in the refectory, where Faculty and students, as in most living rooms of most colleges, mingle. In other words, they are not only co-education but co-eating-and-reading-rooms as well. Then there was the wide campus to look at, the enormous chapel in very fine, very modern Gothic and handsome external stone blocks in two different shades. There was, in fact, an atmosphere of relaxed spaciousness and calm elegance which clearly demonstrated that it was not one of these Life-Adjustment institutions.

Then there was the Whitman exhibition, and as Walt Whitman has been my passion and one of the four or five mystical great-uncles standing round my bed at my intellectual coming-of-age, I wanted to spend time there and stare at those manuscripts in which, whatever the poem is about, whether it is a complex paragraph of the "Song of Myself" or one of those endless lists (which I nevertheless love) of "I see the carpenters with their hacksaws," etc., he rewrites and crosses out twenty times more than might be thought allowably eccentric if it were the opening lines of "L'Allegro" or ten couplets of "The Rape of the Lock." I must get hold of the book which reproduces these pieces of manuscript of this seeming faker, true genius, all in his enormous circular exhibitionistic handwriting. The volume, I noted, was called on the cover "Some Faint Clues And Indirections," and I created a sensation, pleasant to myself, by being able to repeat the poem in which these words come. I then did get my walk, but only half got the sun. Griffiths walked very fast indeed for four miles with me through the forests of the Duke estates. I then came back and asked if I could see the laboratories of Dr. Rhine, but to my pleasure and gratitude it was finally decided that I was asking if I could see Dr. Rhine himself.

Anyhow, there was Dr. Rhine of E.S.P., and there was a long hour and a half's talk with him about these experiments which, as I have said, I had lately been testing at Las Vegas.

He described his experiments and gave me various pamphlets. Incidentally the way to be One-Up at Duke is to be a volunteer student, extra susceptible to E.S.P. He did not talk about the telepathy series, because that's been going on so long that the extent of the positive tendency has been more or less fixed. What he did talk about was the much more interesting precognition series, the opening experiments with the "Seeing Ghosts" series, and the most puzzling of all, perhaps, which he calls P.K. (for Psycho-Kinesis[1]). Dr. Rhine has enormously thick iron-grey hair bushing out over his forehead, and his restless eyes are far set back beneath a big overmantel of brow. He is rather deaf and still deafer to my English accent. His way of explaining things is most un-Joad-like in its lack of clear-cut-

[1] The power to influence the movement of inanimate objects.

ness; he skips and rambles a little bit in an amused way, but gets there somewhat more clearly in the end. He does not, like some men in his position, impatiently take it for granted that everybody has studied his subject, but is patently delighted that anybody should be interested in it. I gather that the two principal methods most in favour now in the P.K. series are (*a*) to try to make spheres wobble one way or the other on an uneven slope by willing them, and (*b*) to try to make dice, flung electrically and untouched by human hand, come up with one particular face uppermost. The dice are used to keep the flame of personal interest alive in the hearts of Dr. Rhine's vast circle of crap-throwing, American student volunteer helpers. He scribbled graphs on a bit of paper. "One series is leading to a result which is beautifully inexplicable," he said. He was amused by the little graph line he was drawing at the moment. "We have found that when the will is fresh the results are positive; in other words, there is a measurable tendency for the dice to fall with the desired face upwards. But Philadelphia spent a year on this problem and they have found an interesting corollary. When the will is tired——" He hesitated.

"Nothing happens?" Dr. Rhine was drawing a dipping curve. "Back to fifty-fifty?"

"On the contrary, the thing seems to work in reverse. . . . The results work actually against the attempt of the will. Do you see?"

I did. I was thinking of that big wheel, at 4 a.m., in the Solid Emerald, and that horrid little quiver as it skipped past my number, when I came back for my second, unsuccessful, effort.

"And, of course, there's no explanation?" I said.

"Well, that's not really our province. All I can tell you is that the tendency is confirmed in a series we have carried out ourselves."

It would have been stupid to mention my little experience at Las Vegas—to speak, as if it were some kind of confirmation, about my series-of-one, vaguely observed, by myself alone, to a man who works on percentages evolved from a series of the order of 100,000, carried out in laboratory conditions.

The more we talked the more interested I became. Dr. Rhine told me how his researches started. It was when he was working under the greatest of all American psychologists, Macdougall, that he heard a lecture given by Conan Doyle on spiritualism. Although it was recognised that this was the great man's little weakness, though most of it was obviously nonsense and very little of it scientific in its approach, there were certain elements and sentences spoken by this revered and loved author which made Rhine think: "Let's see if any of this is susceptible to *scientific* evaluation . . . the element of clairvoyance, for instance, or telepathy." I felt I had been in the presence of a true deductive scientist, who did not force his observed data into preconceived patterns. A Galapagos-Islands, orbit-of-Mercury scientist.

*　　　*　　　*　　　*

My last lecture, to a big audience, was as pleasant for me as any I gave. At the beginning I explained my long-term life-manship motive, as I call it, in going to Las Vegas—so that I could be One-Up on that little casino in Juan-les-Pins when I next went to the South of France. But, I said, by its superior attitude and better understanding of chance and the law of averages, Duke University, with its brilliant E.S.P.manship, could be said to be one up on Las Vegas. The audience laughed; and then before the laugh was over, what I had said was repeated to the slightly deaf Dr. Rhine. He laughed the fraction late, ESP in reverse.

Unwary students asked me to drink beer with them in Durham afterwards, and found it difficult to get rid of me, so full was I of advice on How to be a Writer, How and Where to Travel in Europe, What to Choose for a Career.

18*th November*. My 7.55 a.m. plane from Durham gets into La Guardia in time for me to taxi north to Idlewild, but I have an irritating wait while Transatlantic TWA catches up with itself for a take-off at 4.40 which lands at Shannon about fifteen hours later in a very cold morning light. The TWA pilot miraculously finds his way through the only hole in the clouds which leads straight down to the damp runway. My first realisation that this is Europe and not U.S. springs from the fact that the Irish workmen, sweeping the asphalt, instead of being in well-cut workmen's overalls, are in pre-war, fourth-hand, old overcoats of napless black. I am so stuffed with unexpressed gratitude for the hospitality, almost completely unreturned, of my American hosts, that, finding a young, modest, shy American couple who are making their first visit to England and Europe, I unloaded on them such a torrent of helpful advice and wild offers to take them to hotels, introduce them to bankers, etc. (their name was Plympton), that they thought I was a con. man. I shared my taxi with them, paying more than my share (only a little more) from London Airport to Sloane Street. I was ashamed that they should be plunged so soon into damp November suburbs and the dingy-cute factory architecture and bottle-necks of the Great West Road, which (the driver of our extremely unluxurious limousine explained proudly to the U.S.) "has got three traffic-lines." To recover I steered them off route past Hogarth's house and Chiswick Mall. Unfortunately the Thames had such a low tide that the water was drawn back far enough to exhibit the vast unsavoury details of the river's toothless old gums, and not even a couple of dirty swans, not even Bedford House, made up for the dead-weight of dying autumn.

I still have to put another seventy miles on to my 17,000, or whatever it is, because H. is already at the S.'s, near Salisbury, for our week-end, waiting for me. I drove the distance briskly. I wish my two young U.S. friends could have seen my host's beautiful seventeenth-century house and known how it looked to me, and how his wine tasted to me, that evening at dinner.